M

By David Scherer Water

A GUIDE FOR NEWCOMERS, TOURISTS,
LONG TIME RESIDENTS OR REALLY ANYONE
WONDERING HOW THINGS GOT TO BE
THE WAY THEY ARE

Illustrations by Arrington de Dionyso

For Shannon Wianecki, the spark.

First edition November 2017
Second edition August 2018
Third edition February 2019
Fourth edition December 2022

Making sense of the place where you live is an essential first step if you want to change it. In that regard, making sense of a place is a kind of activism.

In exchange for your trust, I'll be mostly giving you a straight history, but if you know me, you know I can't just let the local absurdity, accidental poetry or inadvertent humor go by without joining in the fun. So, there's going to be some of that. I'm going to match your trust with my own and trust you'll be able to tell when I'm employing a little color, exaggeration and hyperbole to help reveal the deeper truth.

When you're done reading, there will still be parts of Olympia that won't make sense to you. You may even be more confused than when you started. That's okay. Olympia may never make sense to you, or anyone else. Making sense of Olympia is an ongoing process.

This is not a work of fiction. Names, characters, places and incidents are not products of my imagination. Resemblance to actual events, locales and persons, living or dead, is entirely intentional.

–DSW

ABOUT THIS PLACE

During the last 15 decades, larger cities have threatened to steal the state capital from Olympia. On two occasions this fight went all the way to Washington's supreme court. Both trials were long and came down to close decisions.

Surrounded by hungry wolves from the start, it's no wonder that anxiety is woven into the fabric of life here. This is seen in countless campaigns to seem like the best place on earth. Recently the city's motto was changed to include "Olympia, Capital of Washington State."

There's no better manifestation of Olympia's anxiety than the racks at the Olympia Visitor Information Center. The shelves are so crowded with glossy advertisements, brochures, guides and chamber of commerce propaganda that you'd think Olympia was a major metropolitan city.

I believe the capital is secure, that it's time for Olympia to put aside defensiveness. With that in mind, what follows is a step in this direction, an honest look at the real Olympia, an outline of the unique, weird, sad, beautiful, good, bad and funny parts of this place and a few theories on how it all came to be.

INTRODUCTION

For most of the last 500 million years, Olympia was under the ocean. Only recently (the last 80 million years) has this part of North America had a chance to dry out.

Above the sea, it hasn't been a smooth ride. During the last 2.6 million years, the Cordilleran Ice Sheet (a million square miles of mile-high ice) made dozens of passes over the Pacific Northwest. The last time Cordilleran backed up, about 20,000 years ago, it carved out the Puget Sound. What's most peculiar about these repeating scrapes with big ice is how each time, the furthest southern point, the place where the ice wall inexplicably stopped, was Olympia.

What force prevented the ice from plowing south into Oregon and California? This remains one of geology's greatest unsolved mysteries. Today, a shuttered Baskin-Robbins on the corner of Custer and Capitol marks the spot where the massive glacier stopped. Theories range from salt in the soil to the effects of the sun. A folk legend tells of an anti-ice spell cast by the last Mima mammoth. Some say that spell still lingers, explaining Olympia's high standing in national barista and roller derby competitions.

One thing's for sure, whatever stopped the giant glaciers didn't stop a rampage of terrifying white people. By the middle of the 19th Century, thousands of indigenous people were being hunted or moved to internment camps to make way for forts, fences, streetlights and strip malls. And, when the first settlers ran out of arms-reach natives, they turned on each other.

White-on-white violence dates back to 1846 when Olympia had a white population of two. It was Levi Smith and Edmund Sylvester, Olympia's original odd couple. The two divided the city 50/50 and were getting along just fine. Well, fine until '48 when Smith had a "canoe accident" and "drowned" and Sylvester "got" all his land. Over the subsequent decades, Sylvester generously gave large tracts to his new "friends" as he named, platted and effectively created the city we have today.

This kind of suspicious generosity continues.

Olympia is home to a large population of over-educated creative Caucasians offering bounties of difficult to gauge satires and ample helpings of passive aggression.

There are countless natural wonders in these 19.69 square miles. You'll find rolling hills, bubbling artesian springs and beaches of gravel, sand and mud. Best of all, this stuff is never far. Roughly eight percent of Olympia is a city-owned public park. In these several thousand acres, rich and poor freely smell the sweet perfume of flowers, listen to the wind rustling through the trees, and feel the gentle caress of tides, rivers and lakes.

Olympia's unnatural world is equally inspiring. Many don't realize that the land of modern day downtown is manmade. Between 1909 and 1911, Olympia mayor P. H. Carlyon bucketed 2.3 million cubic yards of mud from the harbor to make a great stinking sandcastle. At the time, everyone promised to name his 29-block neighborhood "Carlyon's Fill," but the name never stuck, although it stunk. Carlyon died before it stopped stinking and before his ultimate dream came to be. He imagined Capitol Lake fifty years before it was created.

Today, the stateliness of Washington State's Capital (and its capitol) are reflected in its reflection pool, mysteriously named Capitol Lake. The lake is a fitting flourish to the boob-bomb behemoth up on the hill. The western hemisphere's largest all-masonry dome is made from 1,400 pieces of unreinforced sandstone and visible from some of the furthest points in Thurston County.

Before the dome was erected, and before Carlyon's reshaping of downtown, the small peninsula that separated the east and west bay of Budd Inlet appeared from high ground to resemble the profile of a bear and may be why the earliest names used by Lushootseed natives included TuxustcE'ltûd (a phrase that means "land of the bear"). Today, to the north, another bear profile shape, perhaps the mother bear, is made by the larger peninsula that extends from Priest Point (the bear's paw) to Boston Harbor (the bear's nose).

Perhaps a better name for the city today would be Land of the Drink. Olympia somehow sustains a whopping eighty-three financially solvent bars. Forty-one of these are downtown. How can a city with a population under 50,000 sustain that many bars? No one can explain this mind-boggling feat, nor can they explain how Olympia is able to sustain over forty tattoo shops, thirty-one Asian food restaurants, and fifty-eight banks. Yet somehow this all flows seamlessly in the dance that is the Olympia business scene.

Despite its prestige and fame, Olympia is small compared to other cities. In the State of Washington there are 23 cities bigger than Olympia. In the whole United States 749 are larger. Less than 3% of Olympia's population lives in the area commonly referred to as the downtown core, which is why the majority of the people seen downtown are visitors.

Late night activity in downtown has been steadily growing. Bars, restaurants, performance venues and late night places offer dress-up destinations. Following a trend that started roughly ten years ago, the downtown evening economy may soon be stronger than the daytime one.

Olympia is the home of Evergreen. In 1967 when the alternative college opened, the 1960s still hadn't reached quiet Olympia where things were still very much like they had been in the 1950s. The cultural shift that Evergreen caused was seismic. Evergreen made Olympia a globally known counterculture hot spot. The college continues to draw strange people, many of whom have become permanent residents and have integrated into the Olympia establishment.

If Olympia was overly serious about itself before Evergreen, the effects of higher education intellectualism and privilege doubled it. What is the revolution being led by entitled white people? How do we make fun of this kind of social justice stereotype without punching down? Who knows? Maybe you can't? When talking about Olympia's counterculture it's important to always end your sentences with question marks? Question everything? Always? Yes?

For at least a hundred years, there have been people in Olympia who identified as anarchists, but in the last decade the number has skyrocketed. The term "anarchist" has meant different things to different people at different times. A study of the history of anarchism in Olympia would be helpful, but either they didn't keep records or their records were lost, suppressed or destroyed. Presently the general defining trait of Olympia's anarchists is a resistance to definition.

And, let's not forget The Ramtha School of Enlightenment, by far Olympia's greatest contradiction. To some, it's the spiritual sanctuary they've searched for their whole lives. To others, it's a humiliating implausible racist pile of shit.

There's far more to get to.

Welcome to Olympia.

Let's dive in.

There's an unfortunate history of white people writing about Native Americans in a way that promotes a false mythology, one that bypasses the hard to face truth. In writing this section, I made efforts to overcome that tendency, met with local tribal leaders and tribal historians, and had this section vetted. What follows is not a comprehensive history. For that, I encourage you to visit the Squaxin Island and Steilacoom Tribal museums, to which I am grateful for their assistance and generosity.   -DSW

FIRST PEOPLE

Native Americans are living here still. It's a myth that they're long gone. They have lived in and around Olympia for the last 12,000 years.

Today, South Sound tribal communities are thriving, and given the centuries of violence, persecution and prejudice, this is no small miracle. Tribal communities maintain cohesion through cultural celebrations and political will through remarkable organizing. In recent years, tribal influence has been a check on failed state environmental protections and a challenge to the corrosive effects of private sector development.

Before white people invaded the South Sound, countless generations of first people inhabited the region in large and small tribal villages, enjoyed the rich natural resources and used Olympia as a meeting place and seasonal camp. Life expectancy was above one hundred.

Tribal identity was more fluid before white settlement. Today, for reasons related to pushing back against assimilation and operating within the U.S. federal recognition system, regional native communities are organized into more formal tribes. These include the Suquamish, Duwamish, Nisqually, Snoqualmie, Squaxin Island, Steilacoom and Muckleshoot; however, these modern tribes are themselves collections of former smaller tribes, villages or families.

In 1800, the thousands of natives living in and around Olympia spoke a dialect of the Puget Sound Salish language, Lushootseed. They lived in villages often of just one or two large rectangular houses with a single sloping roof and walls of split cedar boards covering carved post and beam frames. Each house was home to an extended family or to groups related by marriage, under the leadership of an individual.

A house was multipurpose and often used as a workshop where fishing and hunting gear was constructed and mended, where canoe carvers worked on the beach just outside, and where weavers and basket makers created clothing, utensils and artwork from roots, colored bark, grasses, the wool of mountain goats and the fur of dogs.

During the warmer months, much of the focus was on acquiring the physical resources needed to survive. Individuals and groups came and went from villages. Canoeing and running were the primary forms of transportation. [1] Strips of cedar bark were harvested from huge standing trees in the spring, when it could be pulled away easily for use in clothing and baskets.

In summer, the mountain passes could be crossed for trading with friends and relatives to the east. Loaded canoes traveled between river and saltwater villages. Hunting expeditions pursued elk, deer, seal, bear, duck, and other prey. Shellfish were harvested on beaches and mud flats. During salmon runs a large part of a village's annual food supply was acquired within a few weeks.

The colder months were a time for an important, yet less tangible wealth, the ancient legends and ceremonies handed down through generations. Songs and dances were the visible manifestation of a relationship with the supernatural world. Winter gatherings were a time when marriage ceremonies occurred.

At the heart of winter traditions was the telling of syayahub ("syah-yah-hobe"), legends for the education of young people and enjoyment of adults. Through an oral literature given as short vignettes, epics, or cycles of stories, lessons were passed down about the origin of the world and its inhabitants, about ancient monsters, natural phenomena, animal behavior, morality and culture.

It was into this intricate civilization of interrelated villages and families, of resources managed with a light hand, that the first Europeans entered. In 1792, Peter Puget and his exploring party were the first white people to come to Olympia. After Puget, other explorers came through, but it wouldn't be until 1832 that the first white people stayed, setting up a trading post near Steilacoom at the Sequalitchew Tribal Village on behalf of the Hudson Bay Company. [2]

Thirteen years later, in 1845, a young Nisqually tribal leader named Leschi discovered Michael T. Simmons and his friends, starving, lost and stuck in the mud. The group had trekked all the way from Missouri to take the first land claims in the region now called Tumwater.

The Simmons party would never have survived their first winter without Leschi bringing them supplies or the Steh-chass village located at the base of the falls offering them one of their longhouses. This kind of generosity was (and still is) the hallmark of native communities in and around Olympia.

The early settler period was marked by an escalation of injustices directed at natives for whom there was no recourse. In 1854, while visiting, Tlingit tribal leader Tsus-sy-uch was shot dead by Olympia steamboat captain John Butler in front of dozens of witnesses just outside Butler's house on the westside. Butler claimed he shot Tsus-sy-uch because he and his tribe were demanding payment for a month of land-clearing work they'd just finished. Butler was of the school that the natives counted as slaves. He spent a night in jail, but was released the next day. There was no investigation or trial, and requests for restitution from the tribe were ignored. As an ongoing insult, there's still a street, creek and a cove on the westside honoring Butler.

In the aftermath of this event, there were attempts to rope the area's indigenous people into a regulated quasi-slave system. A chart published around 1860 details wage standards for "native servants." These included "1 day work = 1 handkerchief; 1 week work = one shirt; one month's work = one blanket."

Less than ten years after the Simmons party was rescued by Leschi and welcomed by the Steh-chass, the relationships between settlers and natives had spiraled into open hostility. In 1856, their kindness was largely forgotten and the "Puget Sound Indian War" began.

One of the first actions was walling off 4th Avenue in downtown Olympia with a log palisade, making the northern peninsula a fortified safety zone. This was one of many orders to come from a freshly imported territorial governor, the Napoleonesque Isaac Stevens, forefather to good numbers of agro white dudes. [3]

Stevens declared himself Superintendent of Indian Affairs and went around the region on horseback attempting to get natives to sign over claims to their land. When tribes wouldn't sign, or didn't understand his treaties, Stevens escalated hostilities, burned bridges and responded to criticism with a promise that, "the war shall be prosecuted until the last hostile Indian is exterminated."

Over his six years in Washington, Stevens' treatment of Natives prompted pleas for moderation. These came from Olympia residents and across the continent from the Secretary of State and the President.

Stevens' so-called "battles" were one-sided bloodbaths that unleashed a brutality unprecedented in this part of the country. In one of the darkest examples of gruesome irony, Stevens manipulated facts, turned Leschi into a scapegoat and had him hanged. [4]

In the aftermath of his "Indian War" and his departure [5] laws were passed requiring documented native workers wear special blue and red uniforms when in Olympia. Squaxin Island became a forced relocation area and one of history's saddest jokes, The Medicine Creek Treaty was falsely advertised in local newspapers as having been, "ratified by 633 duly authorized Indians who were all satisfied…"

It's not clear if anyone who signed the treaty had any idea what it actually said. It was written in English and crudely translated into the Chinook jargon, a trade language with a vocabulary of few hundred words that was thoroughly inadequate for conveying the complexity of a treaty. Compounding this, there were reports of different versions of the treaty. One promised health care, education and unrestricted access to fish and wildlife resources. Another version promised the Black Hills as a reservation.

In the end, the tribes surrendered over 4,000 square miles and during the years immediately following Medicine Creek, new laws were passed forbidding Native religious practice and inter-tribal trade.

It's a myth that fighting for their rights is a recently started effort. As early as 1897, tribes were appealing through legal channels for fair treatment. One of the main pathways for justice related to the fishing rights promised in treaties. In the mid-1960s these efforts made it onto the national news as a major political awakening was occurring. In some ways, "The Fishing Wars" as they were known in Olympia, were what bussing was for African Americans during the Civil Rights Movement.

The leader of this movement was Billy Frank Jr. He was arrested over fifty times for his dedication to the treaty fishing rights cause. Decades of discrimination and ignored treaties were brought to light by his leadership, activism and perseverance.

In 1974, the landmark Boldt Decision finally secured the rights of tribes as promised in treaties that had been ignored for over a hundred years.

The tribes involved benefited greatly from Boldt. Prior to the ruling, natives collected less than five percent of the statewide salmon harvest, but by 1984, this had increased to forty-nine percent.

Part of the genius in this arrangement related to cooperative management through the Northwest Indian Fisheries Commission. Billy Frank Jr. served as its chairman for over thirty years.

Frank died in 2014. The Nisqually Wildlife Refuge was renamed in his memory.

There are wrongs that still haven't been repaired. There are tribes still seeking compensation, land and adherence to long-ignored treaties. It's a good idea for visitors to remember they are walking on the stolen land of a people who have been displaced, but not wiped out. While the tribes are thriving, this chapter of history hasn't ended or been reconciled.

---

1. Staying in shape was practically a law in pre-settler times. However, things weren't as lovey-dovey as many Hollywood movies suggest. Slavery, raiding, kidnapping and war were a part of life back then. In addition to outrunning enemies, natives practiced dance as a defensive martial art for repelling attacks. **2.** History remembers The Hudson Bay Company as having a friendly presence near Steilacoom, providing blankets and guns to all, but as you follow the increase of white settlers that come after, there was an escalation of hostility. This is an important first instance of passive aggressive behavior that would continue as a hallmark of the dominant culture in the Pacific Northwest. **3.** Having experienced violence as witness, victim and perpetrator in the Mexican-American War, Stevens arrived in Olympia freaked-out, traumatized and angry. During his time as governor he received appeals from residents and from across the continent from President Pierce and President Lincoln asking him to scale back on the crazy. **4.** On December 10, 2004, a Historical Court of Inquiry following a definitive trial in absentia stated that Leschi was wrongly convicted and executed. (Even if he had killed anyone, it would have been in the theater of war and besides, but there was no proof of this.) **5.** Stevens never enacted his master plan, which involved moving all of western Washington's natives onto a single reservation. He left Olympia in 1861 to lead hundreds of Union soldiers to their death in several gruesome Civil War battles. At the Battle of Chantilly, seconds after picking up a fallen flag and charging up a steep hill, he was shot in the head and died instantly.

CHINESE HISTORY

Olympia's first settlers didn't all come from back east. Some came across the Pacific. The first Chinese immigrants in Olympia played an important role in the cultural and economic life of the city. They opened the first produce markets, laundries and restaurants.

Olympia's first Chinatown was located along the south side of Fourth Avenue between Capitol and Columbia, presently the area surounding The New Moon Café. By the 1890s, Chinatown had migrated to the area around Heritage Bank between Fifth Avenue and Legion. By 1913, it was along Water Street near the Olympia Supply parking lot.

By the last quarter of the 19th century, economic decline was making life hard for everyone. People were frustrated and looking for easy scapegoats. Between 1871 and 1886, Seattle, Portland, Tacoma, Issaquah and Tenino had incidents of mob *physical* violence directed at their Chinese residents.

On the morning of February 6, 1886, Olympia's torch lit mobs went around *verbally* proclaiming (i.e., screaming) that the Chinese needed to leave, or else. This vocal-only mob was actually arrested, jailed and each person was fined $500. At the time, Olympia took pride in its comparatively consequential treatment of its angry white mob, and this was considered refined and progressive for that era. It's important to remember that Chinese immigrants who worked for next to nothing had built a great deal of Olympia's infrastructure, railroads, streets, pier and harbor.

In 1886, there were about 200 Chinese people living in Olympia, a tenth of the total population. Most of them left after the riot, walking out on the tracks they built.

In the early days of the city there weren't many African American residents and the few who came weren't warmly welcomed. At least Olympia wasn't passing laws like Portland's which promised bi-annual public whippings of "any free blacks found guilty of staying longer than six months." Oregon's relatively racist atmosphere encouraged two of Olympia's pioneers, George Bush and Rebecca Howard, not to linger there and come north.

In Olympia, both were granted special rare exceptions and allowed to own property. Bush's generosity and ingenious farming practices saved countless early settlers from starvation. In 1876 Bush's sons put Washington agriculture on the national stage in Philadelphia at the U.S. Centennial Celebration by winning first prize for grain cultivation.

Rebecca Howard owned and operated The Pacific House, a hotel on State Avenue where President Rutherford B. Hayes was a guest in 1880. Today the site includes a mural honoring Olympia's early African Americans. A nearby City park was named for Howard in 2022 [6].

---

6. After Rebecca Howard's death, the Pacific House and its neighborhood transitioned into Olympia's red light district, affectionately known as The Restricted District or Tenderloin. The area was home to several brothels and colorful characters including Big Bill McGowan, a large bruiser and small time boxer who ran all manner of vice at his Green Tree Saloon that was a popular spot for the earliest members of The Olympia Lowlife. Today this site is a parking lot adjacent to an erotic bakery called The Bread Peddler.

WOMEN'S HISTORY

As is typical of history, not a lot is known about the lives of Olympia's first female settlers, especially the poor and working class ones.

Washington was a leader in women's suffrage and its campaign was centered in Olympia. Ann Bigelow was a key player and hosted Susan B. Anthony at her house on Glass Avenue. Mary Olney Brown was an Olympia area activist who organized women to break the law and vote in the election of 1870. Her own ballot was rejected, but ballots cast by women in other parts of Olympia made it into the official tally.

Despite not being allowed to vote, women could hold public office. In 1871, Pamela Case Hale was the first woman elected to a State office. Twenty years later, she was the wealthiest person in Thurston County.

In 1910, Washington became the fifth state to allow women to vote, ten years before the rest of the country.

In 1953, with the appointment of Amanda Benek Smith, Olympia became the first U.S. capital city to have a female mayor. The first female Mayor to be directly elected by the voters didn't happen until 2016 with the election of Cheryl Selby. Selby made history in 2020 by becoming the first two-term mayor in Olympia history.

In 1984, Olympia hosted the time trials for the historic first Olympic women's marathon.

Today, Olympia is on the front lines in the ongoing mission for equality, and significant progress has been made in creating room for residents to explore their personal definitions of gender. [7]

---

7. Just because people have radical opinions or an innovative lifestyle, doesn't mean that gender inequality isn't alive and well in most peoples' day-to-day existence. Despite a widespread understanding of feminism and contrary to hippie positivity, women in Olympia experience sexual assault, eating disorders, tend to take on more of the work of parenting than men, are the targets of gossip, experience being shamed for not being political enough, not being artistic enough and not wearing fashionable outfits. In group conversations, women in Olympia are talked over or interrupted more often than men. That said, it's important to mention that there's another side to this. While complaining is a favorite pastime among long time residents, newcomers are often surprised by the thoughtfulness that is frequently taken for granted. When people move away, they're often shocked by how dogmatic other places still are.

JAPANESE HISTORY

Not a lot is known about Olympia's first Japanese settlers. Around 1850 a Japanese ship sank off the Washington coast and a small group of survivors are rumored to have settled in Olympia. In the decades following, Japanese immigrants worked in local fishing, lumber and railroad construction. All U.S. immigration from Japan was cut off in 1924 in response to a growing but wholly imagined hysteria of Japanese takeover.

In June of 1942, 13,391 U.S. citizens of Japanese heritage were forcibly moved out of Washington State. [8] Most of those from Olympia were moved to camps in Idaho and near Tule Lake, California. It's important to note that zero of Olympia's far greater population of German and Italian residents were treated in this manner. It's not clear what happened to Olympia's displaced residents. Did they return to their homes and jobs?

It's unknown if there was a deliberate connection between the abuse of Olympia's Japanese residents during WWII and the formation of its sister city association. [9] In 1981, Olympia and the city of Yashiro, Japan started a sister city association. In 1990, Olympia opened Yashiro Gardens as part of the partnership. The city of Yashiro donated a granite lantern to the new garden and renamed its main thoroughfare Olympia Avenue. Olympia responded by donating a wooden sculpture of an orca made by Joe Tougas similar to the one at Percival Landing. In 2004, Olympia named the 4th Avenue Bridge, The Olympia-Yashiro Friendship Bridge.

In 2006, Yashiro ceased to be a Japanese city when it merged with two neighboring towns and renamed itself Kato City. The sister city status remains intact although plaques in Olympia haven't been changed to reflect the new name.

Olympia's Japanese community holds an annual event in August, a Bon-Odori Festival. At the heart of the festival are practices that honor ancestors. Participants set paper lanterns out on the water and join in dances.

---

8. The same week that Olympia residents of Japanese ancestry were removed, the town experienced not one, but two incidents of self-inflicted accidental aerial carnage. First, a small fighter plane from McChord came smoking out of the sky, sideswiped St. Peter's Hospital and crashed to the street in flames. The pilot died in the hospital he partially destroyed. One military policeman helping in the rescue operation was knocked unconscious when he touched a downed power line and deputy sheriff Ed Stearns was (according to the Olympian), "...thrown to the ground by an exploding bullet." The other fatal aerial incident was only a few hours later when a second single pilot plane crashed into the prairie between Olympia and Yelm.
9. Olympia has a lot of sisters. At one time there was a sister city association with Olympia, Greece and with the Uzbekistan city of Samarkand. These are no longer in effect. In August 2010, Olympia started a sister city association with Nanchang, located in southeastern China. In 1988, Thurston County started a sister city association with Santo Tomás, Nicaragua. In 2007 an unofficial sister city association started with the Palestinian town of Rafah.

PROGRESSIVE HISTORY

Near the end of 1851, Daniel Bigelow, a Harvard educated lawyer came west to Olympia where he met and married Ann White. The two were the town's first straightedge punks. They fought for the causes of women's rights, racial equality, universal education and above all, sobriety. [10]

Despite the influence of the Bigelows, for the first hundred years of the city's history, Olympia was overall a conservative place and only occasionally moderately progressive. By 1970, this started to shift in a very big way with the opening of The Evergreen State College.

Today, born almost exclusively from the

gleaming world of higher education, Olympia's progressive communities have a privileged, critical, hypersensitive and intellectual vibe. Sometimes this yields creative and innovative strategies. Sometimes this leads to endless talks, inaction, drama and an inability to sustain or follow through on plans.

---

10. The Bigelow family politics were liberal, but their material conservatism was off the charts. Most of their possession and even their home, built in 1854, are still in good condition. Today the house serves as a historic museum, is open for public tours and offers a glimpse into what life was like for Olympia's middle class residents during the mid-19th Century.

LITTLE HOLLYWOOD

In the early years of the city, there were several patches of land where almost anyone could freely erect a dwelling. These camps were in the least desired places, tidal mudflats and sites that regularly flooded. The most famous one was at the base of Capitol bluff.

More affluent people made fun of the people who lived there by naming it Little Hollywood. Some of the makeshift houses floated on the water during high tide and rested in the mud at low tide. Some were perched on pilings from an abandoned dock. There were many semi-permanent structures and several businesses including the Knutson's blacksmith shop.

Little is known about the families that lived there, however Little Hollywood existed for over forty years. As Olympia moved closer to getting its fancy manmade reflection pool installed, the city ended its tolerance. On September 2, 1942, the Olympia Fire Department set the whole place on fire. As a fascinating coincidence, in the 1930s, the father of Olympia's recently retired fire chief was a resident of Little Hollywood.

I'd like to imagine that there will come a day when we'll all be living like they did in Little Hollywood, closer to the water, closer to the earth, more in line with the way people had lived in Olympia for thousands of years.

PERCIVAL

Captain Sam Percival may have also been a Major and later an Admiral. He owned a good chunk of the westside and commanded Olympia's small navy. In 1860, Percival attempted to take the upper hand with the tides. He was frustrated because for only a few hours a day at the highest part of the high tide could smaller ships load or unload at the port. Larger ships couldn't reach the port at all. Instead of dealing with the narrow tide window, most boats passed their goods into small dinghies to be rowed ashore.

Percival started his war on the tides by naming Olympia's small wooden pier for himself. Soon after, he ordered his band of Chinese quasi-slaves to build it bigger. As legend goes, the pier was destroyed by a flood, Percival got lost in the grip of an acute rage and shouted the now famous Olympia catch phrase, "It's the water!"

Like every other rich guy at that time, Percival couldn't tell where he ended and the things named for him began. He was convinced that both he and his pier were just too small. While he couldn't change his body, he could expand his pier, but even when his enormous landing was extended 4,798 feet into the deepest waters of the harbor, he ordered that it be extended further.

During the Commodore/Captain/Admiral/Major's career, the port went from being able to dock the largest vessels in Puget Sound to being able to handle modern aircraft carriers, none of which existed yet or would ever come to his gigantic pier.

Perhaps Percival imagined Olympia as some kind of new New Amsterdam where mile-long boats would be dotting the sound. By 1919 ships requiring his pier still didn't exist and later that year, during an earthquake after decades of being gnawed at by teredo worms, his pier collapsed. Percival's corpse can be heard thrashing in its coffin every time the city converts his landing for boats into more of a charming park for people.

Today, Percival Landing is a pressure-treated timber-planked boardwalk and home to a forty foot manual centrifuge for children, coin operated showers that take debit cards, a twelve foot pregnant obelisk, a time travel tidal pool replica made of granite that includes a frightening sign describing the dangers of the fountain's toxic waters and on the northeast end you'll find dozens of locked restrooms. It's not known if there are toilets or sinks inside. The Port of Olympia claims keys are available for day-use marina slip users, but there aren't any day-use marina slips there.

If you visit Percival Landing at night beware of the newly installed recessed ground-level LED spotlights. They're blinding.

WOHLEB

Many of Olympia's older buildings have similar unique flourishes that include terra cotta Spanish roofs and stucco walls set with occasional glazed accent tiles. Architecturally, this isn't anything great, but the story of the guy who conned his way into designing them all is.

For three years, young Joseph Wohleb had been living in his parents' basement in Vallejo, working as a carpenter's assistant and hating life. After looking over the shoulders of architects visiting his job site, Wohleb figured he could do that too. So, he left home and dropped anchor in Olympia.

On April 12, 1911, The Olympian wrote of his arrival, "J.H. Wohleb, architect from California, arrived in Olympia Wednesday. Mr. Wohleb has been making specialty residence, being familiar with the various bungalow styles so popular in California."

Young Wohleb, had no license, let alone experience, and only "self-identified" as an architect. Locals took a risk. He built a few houses. He told everyone they were fancy, and by some miracle they didn't fall over. Over the next few years he was commissioned to do a few buildings. It wasn't long before he was the most sought after architect in the region and his style became ubiquitous.

Wohleb's big break came in 1920 when he won the contract to build the Lord Mansion (now a downtown event space for Evergreen). Over the next three decades, Wohleb did The Spar, several schools, including Lincoln and Avanti, the Capital Theater, the (former) County Courthouse, The Martin and most of the buildings around it.

Wohleb's architecture was sound and a lot of it remains standing. His firm was taken over by his son, changed names a few times and still exists today.

YOUTH CULTURE

Some of Olympia's most commercially
successful visual artists have made fortunes
presenting sugarcoated depictions of counterculture
family life. Contrary to this conception, parents in
Olympia regularly experience despair,
poorly behaved children and a few of them aren't
visual artists.

Olympia has been a laboratory for
unconventional and experimental parenting.
Awesome, horrible and complicated are among the
wide-ranging terms used by people when
describing their experience of growing up here.
Many have grown up fast asleep in a protected
garden dreamland. Others have grown up too fast
and too awake. Others were raised to be weapons
challenging the status quo.

The desperation to get away from home isn't a
given among Olympia youth. In a curious reversal of
norms, it's not uncommon for young people to
remain in Olympia well into their adult lives.

Olympia has been home to some young people
who have confidently moved out of the circles
where young people typically have
influence. There's no better example than Rachel
Corrie. A graduate of Capital High School, she went
on to become an internationally famous peace
activist and died in Israel trying to prevent the Israeli

army's demolition of a Palestinian house.

Rachel Corrie may be the most widely known, but she isn't an anomaly. There are large numbers of world-changing, Olympia-raised young people.

BLACK LIVES MATTER

Interactions with the Olympia Police Department rarely result in violence. However, every once in a while they do. Some of these instances have been criticized for excessive force and/or racial bias. When Danny Spencer died in police custody in 1989, his only crime was an unpaid parking ticket. Stephen Edwards was tasered to death for shoplifting in 2002. José Ramirez-Jimenez was shot and killed by Olympia police during a traffic stop in 2008.

On May 21, 2015, an incident involving OPD sent shockwaves through the city. Two unarmed young African-American men, André Thompson and Bryson Chaplin, were shot in the back during an encounter with Officer Ryan Donald near Cooper Point Road. Donald had stopped the men because they matched the description of suspects who had allegedly stolen beer from a nearby Safeway.

Officer Donald has a history of violating police conduct policy and has been disciplined and counseled about going into situations without appropriate back up. He remains employed with OPD and received over $35,000 in wages and benefits while suspended during the investigation.

This wasn't Officer Donald's only incident involving a questionable use of force on an African American. He was one of six officers involved in an incident in May 2014 when an African-American employee of Century Link was detained at gunpoint. In this case, the city is being sued for $1 million.

In June 2017, Bryson Chaplin and André Thompson were found not guilty of second-degree assault (an offense that involves physical violence), but were found guilty of third degree assault (an offense that doesn't involve physical violence, and in this case, involves causing a police officer to feel apprehension).

After nearly two years of litigation, it was decided by Judge Erik Price that after frightening Officer Donald and being shot in the back by him numerous times, the two brothers should be sent to prison; Thompson for two months and Chaplin in his wheelchair for ten.

This further shattered a local perception that this progressive city is above police brutality or injustice. The trial and its tragic ending have become a focus for organizing the effort to address systemic racism found in police departments in Olympia and everywhere.

In June 2020, following the police murder of George Floyd, Olympia had dozens of protests. In the first few days, OPD, like many other police departments, went overboard. Peaceful protests were treated to concussion grenades, pepper spray and rubber bullets.

Public outcry over these overreactions caused OPD to shift to the opposite extreme. In the first week of July, OPD observed without interruption or arrest, a late-night group of protesters smashing windows. In classic Olympia ironic style, the smashed windows were at one of Olympia's few black-owned businesses.

CRIME

Olympia's overall low crime rates stand in contrast to the city's early history of lawlessness. The first government of the territory had to crudely force civility onto the frontier town with the guns of its pioneer militias. Later, the capitol and the surrounding buildings were designed with excessive marble and intimidating architecture as a push back against the wild west wildness that tormented the city well into the twentieth century. Tour guides at the towering dome of the legislative building tell visitors that it was erected as a celebration of democracy, but older locals remember when it gave everyone a sense of where things were hopefully heading.

Olympia doesn't have a high bank robbery rate,

but because of a few infamous bank robbers, there's a common misconception otherwise. For example, in between bank heists, Eric "The Pizza Time Bandit" Collier got his name robbing local Pizza Time restaurants.

Once convicted, Olympia bank robber Mitchell Rupe famously gained hundreds of pounds in jail, eventually exceeding the scale limit (425), a weight that initially prolonged his life. Rupe had been given the death sentence, but a judge overturned this because hanging would have likely resulted in decapitation, which was considered an illegally cruel, unusual punishment. Before alternate execution arrangements could be agreed to, Rupe died in prison of liver disease related to his weight gain. [11]

America's most prolific bank robber, The Hollywood Bandit (aka Scott Scurlock), was a strikingly handsome Evergreen student turned meth maker. Between 1992 and 1996, wearing elaborate Hollywood style costumes, Scurlock stole 2.3 million dollars and broke and still holds the U.S. record for the longest sequential string of successful bank robberies: seventeen.

Scurlock spent some of his fortune building an elaborate three-story tree house at his 20-acre west Olympia compound, which included an underground Lex Luthor bunker. A few days after his eighteenth bank robbery, Scurlock shot himself in the head during a standoff with police following a hampered getaway snarled by Seattle area traffic.

Statistically and in terms of the general vibe, Olympia is a safe place. Parents let their children wander, doors are left unlocked and some visitors feel like the overall climate is reminiscent of a more innocent time.

Oddly, Olympia's highest crime statistic is its car prowl rate, one that's nearly double the national average. For this reason, OPD encourages car owners to not leave valuable in their cars, or as a hilarious prank, fill parked cars with all manner of unwanted junk.

---

11. Washington's Supreme Court recently eliminated the state's use of the death penalty, however for many years death row inmates could choose between lethal injection and hanging. If no choice was made, hanging was the default. Up until September 2018, Washington was the only U.S. State to maintain a gallows.

CHALLENGES

Owing to the arrival of new money and development, especially in downtown, Olympia may be about to lose its identity, character, affordability and charm.

Or, maybe not. Depending on who you talk to, Olympia is about to collapse into total filth or everyone's about to get evicted by gentrification. It's nearly impossible to tell what's really going on. Olympia's limited economic engine competes with its resistance to improvement. These forces hold Olympia hostage.

Several studies indicate that Olympia's

population is rising faster than any other city in Washington. This raises the question, what's it gong to be: more urban housing or more suburban sprawl/deforestation? Urban development in Olympia has been so erratic that for many years it was said to not exist. At the time of the printing of this book, when a new 140-unit apartment opened, some are declaring the dawn of a new era in downtown development. Time will tell.

Whatever gets built will be problematic because of rising sea levels. Downtown will eventually be completely underwater. The city is exploring options and two involve intentional flooding. The so-called Venice Option involves hardening and abandoning all ground floors and paving the streets with ten feet of water. A more boring option involves erecting a sea wall that's higher than the future high tide mark. A third option involves fully abandoning Olympia's estimated 20 billion dollars of downtown real estate, relocating the city center to higher ground and making downtown an underwater sculpture garden for scuba tourists.

Olympia's most famous imaginary problem is parking. Despite widespread bellyaching, downtown Olympia has no real parking crisis. Victims of parking deficiency syndrome are almost always from the big box suburbs or rural places, and have failed to grasp the idea that by definition a downtown is a dense urban core. It's not a mall, it's not a county fair. If there was ample parking in downtown Olympia, it would cease to be a downtown area.

HOMELESS

The care of the city's most vulnerable residents
has reached new lows and the number of people
sleeping on the streets has reached new highs. It's
not clear if there's a comprehensive strategy
to address this. Homeless advocates appear divided
and scattered in their efforts.

A few years ago, Olympia was debating options
for the city's homeless. At the same time, there was
an unrelated debate about a much needed façade
improvement on The Washington Center For The
Performing Arts. The Center (as it's called for short)
ended up with millions in public funds for a facelift
while next to nothing was spent on the homeless.
Today, the Center's drip-free awning provides a
shelter from the rain for many homeless people. [12]

There's nothing particularly terrible, wonderful
or unique about Olympia's homeless population. In
2015, a statewide study claimed there are only 476
homeless people in Thurston County, but it 2018,
that figure had doubled.

What's most striking is the empathy gap in this
progressive compassionate community. Some cities
have ended homelessness. Why not Olympia?

One theory explains how dispensing only a
minimum of social welfare—in the form of a
handful of anemic shelters, aid agencies and one
lovable bicycle-powered used pizza dispensary—

keeps Olympia's homeless alive long enough to play a scapegoat role. In this way, the homeless offer a distraction to Olympia's other problems.

One thing's for sure, Olympia's tired homeless advocates are set up in a grim cycle of support for their work and withdrawal of support for their work. They face fatigue, burnout and even homelessness.

---

12. The Washington Center props up middle-class morale, hosts poorly attended events and other ones that are attended by prodigious numbers of assisted living facility seniors under ticket contract. There are also regular sold-out youth recitals swarming with family obligation zombies. I've pitched ideas to their programming department including: NATURE CONTAINED, a full-stage terrarium, broad-spectrum lighting, and the cast: living plants slowly growing during two ninety-minute acts with one intermission. BATS THE MUSICAL, with actors in harnesses, trapeze, pulleys and ropes; the plot is intentionally uncertain; the score is a series of echolocation tones; vibe like famous musical with a similar name. NIGHT OF MIDDLE C, the most famous note of all played on various instruments for different lengths of time, at different tempos.

MUSIC

Olympia's contribution to the world of music is an important but sometimes touchy subject. Some people speak of it in religious tones. Others feign nonchalance. There are some who say that it's not possible to write an unbiased summary. Well, here goes.

In 1892, on the corner of 4th and Cherry, present

site of city hall, local media mogul millionaire John Miller Murphy built Olympia's first major music venue, a 3-story 1000-seat opera house. John Philip Sousa played, Mark Twain read essays and in grand Olympia style, the behemoth was smashed with a wrecking ball in 1925.

In the years after, Olympia had a typical assortment of small and large music venues and produced music in good quantities. Presumably some of it was just incredible, but none of it stirred the pens of historians or garnered national attention.

That changed in 1959 when for a few weeks, the number one band in America was a trio of youngsters from Olympia. The Fleetwoods would remain Olympia's most widely known contribution to music for the next few decades. During that time there were many imitators and as a result, Olympia's music had a generally bland Fleetwood-esque sound.

On February 26, 1983 a group of local residents rented the vacant space at 211 East 4th Avenue for a one-night performance headlining with Portland punk band, The Wipers. This was unprecedented. Shows like this had always been relegated to basements, living rooms, garages and the Evergreen dorms, with only sporadic moments when bands were permitted to play Skateland, Lakefair or the old Olympia Center. The concept of a dedicated venue for local bands was unheard of. [13]

Riding the excitement over the success of that Wipers' show, The Tropicana was started at 311 East 4th Avenue. While only open for a year, this venue gave the region's young music scene a new confidence and focus. The Melvins, Beat Happening and Girl Trouble played their first shows here. Bands on tour included Black Flag, Slayer and The Butthole Surfers.

While the Olympia Downtown Association had The Tropicana shut down in 1985, something was set in motion that couldn't be stopped. Over the next few years, Olympia's music scene became more substantial. Other venues started, new bands performed, ones that no one had ever heard of before. Among these was a band called Brown Towel. After they changed their name to Nirvana, they changed the world. [14]

Three record labels, Sub Pop, K Records [15] and Kill Rock Stars were started in Olympia. These three would set the stage for a musical revolution. In the 1990s, the Olympia music scene and the feminist movement, Riot Grrrl, were forces challenging the status quo of popular culture and the very definition of music. [16] At its core was a sincerity previously rejected in mainstream youth culture and earlier manifestations of punk rock.

The Olympia DIY music, arts and crafts culture was a celebration of raw honesty and unpolished humanity. The outward fashion was an ironic embrace of 1950s era white bread kitsch. Musical proficiency was shunned and candor celebrated. Outrage directed at the world was tempered by a call for genuine care and love among peers. Olympia challenged cultural and gender stereotypes; women thundered long-held fury; men sang gently of innocence.

For its size, Olympia has been a sanctuary for a large number of artists. This stretches decades and continues today. [17] Fostering this is and has been a culture promoting connection, collaboration, slowing down, an embrace of all that's considered weird in mainstream circles, a rejection of Americanism and its definition of success. The phenomenon is further helped by the fact that Olympia conveniently sits in the shadows of two large cities—close enough for bands to attain financial gain, yet isolated enough to be a retreat, a cool harbor.

Many artists had an important cultivation period in Olympia before going on to bigger things. Nirvana, Bikini Kill, Sleater-Kinney, Unwound, Mirah, Kimya Dawson and Macklemore are examples. However, for every commercially successful band that brewed its groove in the Olympia gloom, or artist who grew their artistic identity in this fertile ground, there are hundreds if not thousands that you've never heard of.

---

13. For decades and continuing today, Olympia's punk houses have remained a place for bands to play all-ages shows. **14.** Taking one's music to larger circles is what nearly all musicians strive for, but for many people, ascending into the highest levels of commercial success can be soul crushing. There's no better example of this than Kurt Cobain. He lived in Olympia for four years, the period when Nirvana coalesced, wrote Nevermind, got signed to a major label and began its rise into mainstream popularity. While few will admit it, almost all musicians dream of having a fraction of the reach Kurt Cobain attained. Love him or hate him, since 1990 he has had a major effect on every Olympia band and individual musician. **15.** In the attic of the former K Records building on the corner of 8th and Jefferson is a small brick casket. Inside there's clay from the Vltava River that was smuggled out of Czechoslovakia in the late 1920's. When the indie music label moved into the building in 2004, they knew the place used to be a synagogue, but knew nothing of the clay that had once touched the hands of Judah Loew ben Bezalel, a late-16th-century rabbi from Prague. For a few months in 2017, the Olympia Pig Bar was in talks to purchase the property, a real nail biter for the Jewish community who had no say in the process. Next-door neighbor Ali Raad purchased the building in 2018 and today the former synagogue turned music label is home to The Christ Our Hope Anglican Church. Which is better, an all you can eat treyf buffet or Christ cult? Yikes. **16.** In the end of the 1980s, the whole world was hungry for integrity and candor, especially in music, and by the middle of the next decade the world had largely swallowed the Pacific Northwest music scene whole with Olympia at its center. Olympia's place at the center has never been widely acknowledged. Most often it's referred to as "The Seattle Music Scene of the 1990s." Perhaps that's for the best. **17.** Bands and musicians with a strong connection to Olympia include Anna Oxygen, Arrington de Dionyso, Bangs, Beat Happening, Bikini Kill, The Blow, Broken Water, C-Average, Chris Sand / Sandman, Christian Mistress, Cool Rays, Lois Maffeo, Dead Air Fresheners, Dub Narcotic Sound System, Earth, Excuse 17, The Family Stoned, The Fleetwoods, The Frumpies, GAG, G.L.O.S.S., godheadSilo, The Go Team, The Gossip, Growing, Halo Benders, Heavens to Betsy, Joey Casio, Karp, Kicking Giant, Kimya Dawson, Lync, The Microphones, Milk Music, Mirah, Miranda July, The Need, Nirvana, Nomy Lamm, The Old Haunts, Old Time Relijun, Rickie Lee Jones, RVIVR, Scream Club, Sleater-Kinney, Some Velvet Sidewalk, Spider & The Webs, Team Dresch, Unwound, Western Hymn, White Boss, Wolves in the Throne Room and госкино. Olympia bands continue to blossom in good numbers, enjoying above average commercial success compared to bands from other cities, and there are occasional predictions of a resurgence of the 1990s era.

SOCIAL STUDIES

Olympia residents spend a good deal of time discussing social dynamics. This was by far the most popular topic that people I interviewed for this book wanted to talk about. With varying degrees of acumen (or plausibility), the following are quotes on this topic.

- "Olympia is a singularity, the last social ecosystem for those who can't exist anywhere else."

- "Some [residents] are so mossed over with local creep that it's difficult to tell the person from the place."

- "Olympia's allergy to mainstream people is only a recent manifestation of decades of prejudice. For the most part, this runs without anyone noticing it, although there have been intermittent efforts to organize foreign exchange programs between mainstream people from Lacey and alternative people from Olympia."

- "The players who define (and enforce) conformity to Olympia's ever-changing counterculture are young adults raised with money but presently presenting as patchwork paupers."

- "Olympia is engrossed in a purity contest with a social hierarchy built on a rickety righteousness ladder. Promotion is awarded for displays of asceticism and pandering to a base of like-minded identity vegans. There's a subsequent rising and falling that creates echoes of victimhood. Cycles of real and metaphorical fasting, paired with prodigious amounts of calling people out, produces one of Olympia's greatest natural resources: tension. The tension shuts people down, or stops events. Radicalized diets (real and metaphor) are adhered to at great suffering, spoiled foods are held as an ideal sustenance, countless tiny jars of sauerkraut are sold at unbelievable prices and grey water is bottled as a kombucha. In secret, hemmed in by mildew and dirty carpets, even stricter diets are designed, complicated protocols are ratified and an unspoken etiquette tightens."

- "Because Olympia has an inordinate number of adults who as children entertained lofty hopes, but today work dead-end jobs, a segment of the long-term population lugs around crushing discouragement as a principal personality feature. This, coupled with a sturdy unwillingness to face the source of it, makes for a robust victim-blame economy circumscribed by smart-sounding psychobabble, and no end in sight. Words like 'systemic' are deployed. By redirecting frustrations at cliché scapegoats, distraction and pseudo-comfort are achieved. However, the tragedy spirals into community spectacle when rolled out in city council or other meetings as the Olympia therapy circus."

- "Is the effort made by so many to not show or act out prejudice intensified by the harsh consequences of doing so? What is the price of social demonization? In some circles, counter-rebellion, an ironic embrace of bigotry, is performed to offset the effect of Olympia's hyper-careful / hyper-harsh class. Is this any better?"

- "Visitors, especially ones from cities with "bad" crime statistics, noticing Olympia's "good" crime statistics make comments about how this masks a general social unsafety, '*I should feel safe here, yet somehow this place just FEELS terrifying. What is that?"*

There are other schools of thought. I could do a whole book on the notes I took during the interviews. There's a seminar happening on every street corner. There are people who will talk your ear off.

ECONOMICS

Olympia's social or political personality may be on par with San Francisco, but the economic situation is another story.

The local economy isn't broken or depressed, it's just one of reasonable proportions. This capital city with a population hovering under 50k has a dependable (but limited) economic engine exclusively fueled by the government of the

13th largest U.S. state. Civil servitude is so far up as number one on the list of Olympia's top 30 employments that if you take the jobs created by the subsequent 29, it still only adds up to less than 30% of the total number of State employees.

Olympia's economic reality is at odds with an excess of cool-ish, young-ish people seeking the kinds of jobs that just aren't here in large enough quantities. So, if you're feeling discouraged by a flagging career track or a low bank account balance, try to remember that it might just be the local economic reality that's making you unhappy, not a personal failing.

Skills that are widespread among Olympia residents are the same ones in shortest supply nearly everywhere else. This fact tickles a moving itch and many residents are perpetually consider moving away.

Other solutions to financial woes include setting lower standards, letting go of world-changing hopes, working a crappy job and renewing efforts, however unlikely, to obtain one of Olympia's few not-so-crappy jobs. Some residents write humorous local history books to help prop up their egos.

Olympia is a small American cake cut into tiny pieces. Until someone discovers gold, oil or really anything, many may not find it satisfying to make a home here.

The inverse can be equally true. Compared to other cities, Olympia has always been a place of rich resources where people making less money can still live a good life. Poorer people in Olympia seem to have more time for relationships, making art, getting involved in activism and taking it easy.

BUSINESS

The gravitational forces exerted by the Interstate (1956) and The Capital Mall (1977) and the weirdening effects of Evergreen (1968) are among the major influences that gave rise to the present ecology of the Olympia downtown business scene. Even before the 1950s, Olympia had a history of being home to some of the strangest stores in the world. Today this continues. Some are born from the counterculture. Others rise from the wild dreams of more mainstream dreamers. Perhaps the most striking thing about Olympia's odd shops is how locals don't blink, and accept it as part of the natural landscape.

Specialty stores are a thing. For over a decade there was a bookstore that only sold murder mysteries. Mario's on 4th Avenue, a popular teen hangout of the 1980s, only sold cigarettes. For several years there was a shop that only sold walking sticks, and another one that only sold tutus. Simply Australian was a shop that only sold items pertaining to Australian culture.

Olympia had not just one, but TWO teddy bear outfitters: Nana Lou's and Bearytale Kingdom. Neither of these stores sold actual teddy bars. They only sold clothing and accessories for your existing ones. Phat Sacs sold used fanny packs and rave survival gear. Bonanza 88 only sold items that cost eighty-eight cents. Druid's Knook sold dusty Celtic figurines and scantily clad fairies titillating on plastic logs. Few pedestrians could pass without reading a proverb changed daily on a Miller Lite dry erase board in the window. Many of the messages had an accusatory tone, such as, "Don't waste your life!"

Olympia's currently still in-business array is remarkable. There is a dermatology clinic for cats. There's a three thousand square foot dog food store. There are pet psychics who offer drop-in sessions at Psychic Sister. With the nearest commercial olive groves over hundreds of miles away, it makes zero sense that Olympia is home to OOO (pronounced "Ooo!"), Olympia's all olive oil emporium.

You'll find comically sloppy institutions with deliberate sloppiness carefully dialed-in to appear accidental. Even at their new location, Burial Grounds has maintained its trademark messiness. If you didn't know better, you'd never guess they've been there for only a short time. Old School Pizza has a men's restroom that looks like the scratch pad in a pen shop and smells like a dragon's urethra.

Drees, Olympia's venerable fancy knickknack store, started in the 1920s when founder Jimmy Drees bought Johnson's Paint and Art. Jimmy soon steered the shop straight into the city's rising population of wealthy homesick East coasters hungry for Manhattan's latest wallpaper patterns and Gatsby-inspired paperweights. Today, not much has changed. The store continues as a overpriced Pier 1.

What accounts for Drees hundred years of steady business? Like many western towns that once represented the edge of civilization, in Olympia one can still hear the echoes of scarcity that plagued the first settlers. It's a curious nagging sensation, a feeling like you're far from the commercial center of the universe. This primordial spell lures locals to Drees' Parisian styled counters with armloads of one of a kind treasures sold by the dozen.

Other shops offer similar wares, but none can claim being at it longer than Drees. It's this seniority that has earned Drees the right to sell a pack of napkins for $540 or a tiny lamp for $1500.

All-Ways Travel has been at their location on the corner of Harrison and Division for forty-eight years.

Is this the last family-owned brick and mortar travel agency in the world? I don't think they know about the Internet. Please don't tell them. At All-Ways Travel you can arrange your exit out of Olympia in classic style, book passage on the Orient Express, lease a camel in Morocco or hire sherpas for a Mt. Everest ascent. By request, you can still get an old-timey handwritten paper ticket with red carbon triplicates.

If a physical travel agency experience doesn't satisfy you, the vape and e-juice shop next door offers the opposite, a supernatural escape. In 1970, Olympia had seventeen travel agencies and exactly zero vape outlets. As a funny coincidence, today Olympia has SEVENTEEN vape outlets. It's not hard to imagine that soon there will be zero of either.

Vaping, the indoor-friendly alternative to conventional fire-based tobacco enjoyment, was propelled into popularity by Washington's 2005 smoking ban. Since the ban, Olympia has seen vape retail locations skyrocket. Handheld vape gizmos look so much like magic markers that many people mistake vape users for magicians.

The spirit of the Olympia vape community is captured by advertising slogans like, "Ride deep into the yawning chasm of dragoscimitar jaggerage and taste the holy ghost-fog of our kaleidoscopic surrender." It's hard to resist. Olympia's most popular vape flavors include: Thanksgiving, Christmas, St. Patrick's, September, Laundry Day, Pizza, laudanum, desoxyn and p:paimt.

　　With the legalization of Marijuana there has been a massive increase in local marijuana-related relativity. Olympia doesn't have a detour bus affectionately called The Canni-Bus, there isn't a quasi-visible vegetable-based greenish 19-seater Econo-van that leaves the downtown bus station at 420 ppm.

　　Creative Office Furniture, on the corner of Legion and Plum, was home of the "Chair of the Month As Featured on KGY" for many decades. Starting in 1999, a duplicate of the chair shown in the storefront display was placed in the air studio at KGY where local radio celebrity and one-time mayor candidate Dick Pust would talk on-air about his sitting experiences.

　　Olympia has a good history of weird food situations. For fourteen amazing months there was a store that only sold marshmallows. There was a savory section. One of the largest producers of in-flight fresh-frozen fruit cup companies used to be based near the Olympia airport. For several years on 4th Avenue there was a bakery for dogs.

There was a banner in front of Wagner's proclaiming it the best bakery in town. The banner is gone now and their new slogan recommends that you get the best since they do. I don't this is true. Wagner's pallets of glassed-in high-gloss quasi-edible confectionism is only carbohydrated visual art and offers little for the taste palate. They almost redeem themselves at the end of the day when anyone can get a mystery bag for fifty cents. Take a chance?

Other food extruderies source off the lowest rungs of the SYSCO stock. Olympia's hog hoards wolf down dog chow as happily as horsehair. If you're in a bind and there's nothing you can do but go to a restaurant, here's my short restaurant review: Chelsea Farms is the best overall, QB has the best food for the price point; Arepa is the best food cart; La Gitana has the best pizza (they import their flour from Italy); Danang has the best soup, is the best Asian food and they stay open late; and, the iconic Old School gets my award for best fast food, with special points for the local/natural soda fountains.

The Olympia restaurant scene plumbs time in endless space knitting, and the culinary entroudge rolls out like a rope of broken bones boring holes in holy boredom. Perhaps this is why secret cafés have been such a steady phenomenon. The first recorded secret café was in the 1930's outside the Mottman Building on 4th Avenue. It was open daily and sold

tamales made from seagull meat. The Track House
(511 7th Ave. SE) brought secret cafés into their
prime in the 1990s. The Red Horse Café had a good
long run of weekly dinners. In the early 2000s the
health department began an effort to hunt down
secret cafés, but they still exist, typically as one-time
fundraisers.

By the time this book is printed, it's likely that
new generations of businesses have already replaced
those listed. Olympia's strange business ecosystem
appears undaunted in fostering a parade of odd
shops that defy conventional business logic (but are
inexplicably solvent), providing inspiration and
perplexity.

BEER

In 1896, at the base of Tumwater Falls, the first
brewery in Olympia was built at the site of the Biles
& Carter Tannery. It's still there, a medieval looking
building that stands in the shadow of the shuttered
modern brewery complex. Initially it was named
Capital Brewing, but everyone referred to the beer
as "Olympia beer" and soon the name became
officially changed.

During prohibition, the brewery would have
passed away if it weren't for creative alternatives
that included the production of unfermented fruit
juice. They also sold purple cakes of dehydrated
wine and tan cakes of shredded hops. These could be

brought home and mixed with a bottled of mouthwash to create a truly disgusting but perfectly dizzying aperitif.

After prohibition, the company hit the ground running with an advertising claim that the local water was purer than anywhere else. Olympia Beer became one of the most successful beer brands in the world. The operation scrambled to keep up with demand, sprinting through the rest of the century in a persistent state of facility expansion along the Deschutes River.

For seven solid decades beer was the chief industry of the city. New technologies and high-speed conveyor belts allowed barrels to roll out by the millions.

Without much warning, all of it came to a sudden and upsetting halt on June 27, 2003.

It's not true that everyone just stopped drinking beer. That's not why the brewery closed. After passing through a succession of corporate owners, South African Brewing decided the facility was a money pit and ordered the brewery to stop. To this day, conveyor belts and bottles sit in the same position gathering dust. The enormous facility is one of the world's largest indoor ghost towns.

The brewery property is not for sale anymore. Chandu Patel bought it. According to his web site, "Chandu is a visionary beacon and a socio-political powerhouse hotel magnate, born and brought up in India. He moved to the United States in 1974, got an MBA in Industrial Management, developed a keen interest in hospitality, became a hotel tycoon and has made millions of dollars in the business." His plan was to turn the buildings into a bourgeois hotel with companion booze oozery. There are no signs of this happening.

Olympia Beer is still sold in local stores, but Miller brews it in southern California, and Pabst owns the label. Local vestiges of the big beer era include the city's inordinate number of bars. As of the printing of this book, Olympia sustains 83, with 41 of them located in the downtown core.

The lost spirit of the old Olympia Brewery haunts the riverside portion of the campus. Tumwater Falls is an open-air museum owned and maintained by the Olympia-Tumwater Foundation, a tragic philanthropic group with a tear-jerking mission to eternally promote a heritage that is today largely irrelevant.

HERITAGE PARK

What's with all the heritage? Why is Olympia's central park named Heritage Park? There is an enduring belief among residents and lawmakers that something important happened here. What was it? Olympia's history from 1850 to present is surely just a cliché tale of increasing numbers of people moving in, acting like they owned the place, having some trifling hardships, but for the most part having a gay old time. Perhaps "Heritage" refers to the tons of landfill and concrete that reshaped this stretch of shoreline? Or, maybe it's a sarcastic "Heritage," an invitation to imagine what things were like before the so-called pioneers arrived?

The park's features include 39 concrete monuments along "The Arc of Statehood," (there's one for each county). At the southern end of the half-mile trail is a replica of "a typical Western Washington ecosystem," a cluster of shrubs surrounding a muddy area frequented by ducks. The northern end of the trail is the "future site of an Eastern Washington ecosystem replica, an arid butte or bluff" that will presumably be maintained in the winter with high-powered electric hand dryers. [18]

Migrating geese are not allowed at Heritage Park. Grounds keepers regularly scare them off with the use of acoustic grenades discharged from a cardboard cannon.

---

18. Near this future site, at the northwest corner of the lake, atop a spiraling mound, sits a thing that looks like a miniature replica of a druid's sacrificial altar. This isn't here to remind you that many residents are the surviving descendants of a lost race of pagans. It's the monument for a time capsule due to open in the year 2051.

CAPITOL LAKE

At the center of Heritage Park is Olympia's
largest artificial body of water. Finished in 1951,
this 260-acre reflecting pool is a testament to man's
domination over nature and was the final touch on a
capitol construction campaign that spanned five
decades.

Capitol Lake has had problems since it was built.
These include filling up with silt, poor water quality,
flooding, unsafe levels of E. coli, milfoil blooms,
degradation of habitats, blobs of eutrophicant
and Potamopyrgus Jenkinsi, "a New Zealand mud
snail smaller than a grain of rice with a capacity to
reach phenomenal densities." All of these problems

tie back to a single issue: salt water no longer does what it did for thousands of years; flush the place out twice a day. [19]

An agreement was finally struck to dynamite the 5th Avenue dam and return this 260-acre mirror back into an estuary, however the reactionary pro-lake posse that formed to counter the fake lake haters has delayed the project. They say that the fake lake needs to be maintained because it showcases the 258,000 square foot capitol that was quietly incanted in 1923 from 92,000 tons of King County's marble and Wilkeson, Washington's sandstone. The lake lovers say that maintaining the lake is not just about showcasing a physical feature, but what that feature stands for, an era of disgusting construction largesse that will never happen again. Good god, the dome alone weighs over 15,000 tons.

A commission has been commissioned to evaluate the debate. Soon after the first printing of this book, a second commission was formed to evaluate the findings of the first. Both groups include citizens, elected officials, environmentalists, tribal leaders and advocates for the protection of escargot.

In September 2018, Floyd-Snider, a Seattle-based consultant was hired to study various options recommended by the commissions. State lawmakers have approved $4 million dollars to cover the consultation fees.

While it's officially agreed that the lake must go, it hasn't budged an inch.

19. Around the lake are many water fountains. Like the lake itself, none of them work. There's an insect-encrusted footbridge to The Marathon Park Restroom Complex with stainless steel urine troughs (frequently shuttered due to ongoing squabbles over restroom hours and costs). Via a footpath, the footbridge leads to The Deschutes Parkway, named after Capitol Lake's dammed river. Along the parkway, pedestrians may enjoy dual parallel trails, graveled and concreted (gravel for the barefoot, concrete for the shod). There are clouds of bugs to enjoy in great mouthfuls.

TUMWATER FALLS

Tumwater Historical Park sits at the base of the falls. The Deschutes River in its yet-to-be dammed nudity bends around it. Across the river you can see the brick remains of the original Olympia Beer brewery building. At the park you'll find electric lighting, iron barbecues, a plastic playground featuring a crank-powered tram and a binary calculator that mystifies adults, but seems to attract toddlers in good numbers. Due to the high water table of this former floodplain, there's a shoe-wrecking mud field coated in a patina of grass.

Up the hill from the playground is a log shaped shack made of logs that's not much bigger than a box. Legend has it that this primitive structure served as the state's first post office, courthouse and assembly hall where the historic debate on the name of the state was chosen by the flip of a quarter. Today this shack serves as a home for half of what remains of Washington's first wooden fire engine. The other half burned in a fire.

To the right of the shack is a house with a sign explaining that it's a house. Then there's a mile of rusting fence that will lead you to one of the city's worst restaurants, The Falls Terrace. They have no need to serve conventional meals; a spectacular view distracts eaters from what appears to be food-flavored sawdust. Entering the upper level Falls Park is an odd feature, a series of concrete cubes. Some are shaped like boats. This might be a playground.

Next to this is a state run salmon hatchery where one can view the fish from elevated platforms and hear them repeatedly asking, "Why? Why? Why?" During posted hours, a hatchery staffer is there to explain in apologetic tones that it's all a hoax. Unable to swim up Tumwater Falls, salmon were never part of this ecosystem. It's only in the last few decades that a mile-long concrete "ladder" has allowed the fish to reach these manmade spawning grounds. This bizarre use of public funds to complete a contrived natural phenomenon is Olympia's most potent metaphor and something to meditate on as you tour the rest of the park.

The trail rolls downstream and offers many breathtaking views of three levels of waterfalls. At the highest, there's a rock depicting the first non-native co-eds to arrive in the region. Further down there are the remains of a riverside amphitheater, an ancient mill and two hydro-electric plants that at one time provided all of the electricity to the city.

Sitting precariously on the cliffs above the

eastern riverbank, the ruins of the Olympia Beer complex casts a foreboding shadow over the entire park (another metaphor). This is one of many rusting relics that tell the story of technology yielding to the winds of change, succumbing to irrelevance despite public outcries for restoration, and leaving behind ruins that seem strange at first glance.

CAPITAL CAMPUS

Olympia's overbuilt capitol campus was intended to have a civilizing effect on the endemic wildness that plagued the government during the early decades of the state. Today it's a lovely place to stroll if you're seeking solitude. Seventy-four percent of the week, the whole campus sits in lugubrious vacancy.

For a few months each year, during the legislative session, the whole place becomes a bustling beehive. The session is a fair of seriousness, a contrast to the rest of the city and wholly separated from it. Visiting the capitol during the session feels like visiting Wall Street on a weekday, a magical departure from Olympia's sleepy dreamy rainbow vibe. The abruptly ending short session leaves everyone blinking, wondering if it was all just a dream.

According to tour guides, certain parts of the campus elicit recurring phrases such as "weird," "creepy," and "I don't get it." There's no better example than Winged Victory, a WWI monument. The statue cluster depicts God as a twelve-foot sorceress ordering three fresh-faced privates and a nurse into battle.

There are two Vietnam War memorials. One is a traditional wall inscribed with the names of fallen soldiers. The other, located on the southeast corner of the campus, is a commentary on the political folly of this chapter of U.S. history, a series of concrete blocks set as a maze with no clear start or end. To further cement the concrete metaphor, once-flowing water fountains inside the labyrinth have sealed themselves with rust and there's a metal sign bolted to the wall proclaiming, "no playing on or around."

Decorative potato fields surrounding the Vietnam War Memorial maze replaced grass landscaping on the terraced lawns a few years back and are rumored to be a memorial to Olympia's Irish immigrants. The potatoes are donated annually to local food banks.

Just east of the Supreme Court chambers stands a non-native Norway maple tree of zero historic significance. Given that this is not its preferred biome, the tree, estimated to be a little less than ninety years old, is not aging well. It has been actively trying to die with some dignity for at least a few decades. Washington State's powerful pro-life tree lobby has helped ensure that an expensive life support system involving dozens of steel crutches, hooks and cables will keep the wretched tree leafing for another century. Landscapers adjusting the elaborate hardware confirmed that the state has spent hundreds of thousands of dollars on the effort.

The shuttered greenhouse on the northwest corner of the campus is an interpretive commentary on global warming. Across the street from it is a heated bench.

Just behind the State Supreme Court there's a memorial to miscarried justice for officers who were killed on the job. On a clear day, this is an ideal place to view the whole city (or read this book).

This is also the spot where Isaac Ebey floated a new name for the city by five other white settlers who were living nearby. Since none of them could pronounce the Lushootseed name, and since they needed something good for advertising to prospectives back east, the group consented without much fanfare. The city has been named Olympia ever since.

Ebey had a thing for names. He named King County. But, that was about it. He died young, killed serving as a colonel of the territorial militia on Whidbey Island.

His name is missing from the fallen officer memorial.

THE LIBRARY

Olympia is a member of The Timberland Regional Library (TRL), a small inter-library loaning network comprising an area about the size of New Jersey.

The Olympia location is enjoyed by more residents than most people would guess. The average daily door count is around 1600, with peaks above 2500. This is busier than Vancouver's library, which is four times larger and has four times the staff.

Despite very high use, the library is an under appreciated public asset, ridiculed and called a magnet for the homeless. This is another local mystery, one that doesn't reconcile with Olympia's progressive climate. One would think that this place—where people are treated with respect regardless of socio-economic status, where people get free help bridging the digital divide, navigating the rising tides of information and the Internet—would be cherished, supported and more of a priority.

The city owns the building and keeps it on a financial starvation diet. They responded to public outrage over people loitering, sleeping and smoking out front and installed blue metal anti-seating waves. These work like pigeon spikes, but for repelling people.

The bulk of the library's inadequate operational funding comes from property taxes levied throughout its 7,600 square mile region, covering four counties, most of which are economically devastated areas. As the name suggests, library also gets money from the sale of state owned timber.

There is a section of the library that includes books that can be checked out without a library card or having any due date.

The local author section includes this book, CDs, vinyl records and cassettes. There are 2,800 photocopier made zines. Sadly, there are zero hand engraved wax slabs, but the library offers free printing (100 page per week limit), free scanning and free faxing.

"Banning" is a recurrent request from library patrons. Library policy protects challenged titles from removal, but the list of requests may reveal something:

- Mama Ruby by Mary Monroe, for "being definitely R-rated"

- George Washington Carver by Tonya Bolden, for "mocking the non-scientific/spiritual parts of his life"

- The Steel Remains by Richard K. Morgan, for "explicit language and male on male sex"

- To Have and Have not by Ernest Hemingway, for "frequent use of 'N' word"

- A People's History of American Empire: a Graphic Adaptation by Howard Zinn, for "anti-American tones and leftist propaganda."

- Curious George Takes a Job by H. A. Rey, for "illustrations of Curious George smoking a cigar and getting loopy on ether"

- My Heart is on the Ground by Ann Rinaldi, for "being incorrect, stereotypical, and insulting."

- The Lost Girls by Alan Moore & Melinda Gebbie, for "graphic back cover images"

- Star Struck by Pamela Anderson, for "a cover featuring full-length female nude"

- Daddy's Wedding by Michael Willhoite, for "depicting gay marriage in an area of the building that's accessible to children"

The library offers its cardholders free access to streaming resources similar to Netflix, free online education programs, free software and mobile app downloads. The library hosts free events in the early mornings and evenings. These are scheduled outside of normal hours only because during normal hours, the building is almost always above maximum occupancy.

There's regular talk about a coming day when the building will no longer be able to serve the growing community demand. This day clearly passed decades ago. I'm not sure what sorcery is holding this amazing place together.

EVERGREEN

After decades of other Washington cities trying to steal the capital, Olympia's general identity and culture developed a protective disdain towards anything odd. This is why the city lapsed into fits of acute anxiety when The Evergreen State College broke ground out on Cooper Point in 1967. Today there are still vestiges of the once chronic eye rolling and grumbling, but for the most part, Evergreen and its graduates have become part of the Olympia establishment.

In 2017, as college campuses around the world wrestled with the debate over how to address institutionalized racism without censoring free speech, Evergreen found itself in the national spotlight. On campus there had been a series of protests and counter protests. Some of it was thought provoking, some of it was awkward and some of it was embarrassing. Racism has plagued Evergreen no less than any other college, free speech is no easy subject to grapple with and Evergreen, like every other college, is struggling with skeletons and unanswered questions. Tiny as it is, the school continues to make big waves.

Evergreen received a good amount of negative press from Fox News (and similar outlets) during its recent wrestling matches. The timing was unfortunate because the college was already knee deep in financial problems related to a decline in enrollment. Numbers have continued to decline and Evergreen appears close to shooting its president out of a canon. The school recently announced a restructuring that would create several colleges within an Evergreen University.

LAKEFAIR

Lakefair is a five-day celebration for and at Capitol Lake. The event draws an estimated quarter million people who pay tribute to the lake by eating deep-fried glop while riding flashy gasoline-powered amusement contraptions. The event is an annual sacrifice to the grass at Heritage Park. [20]

Lakefair draws regular but feeble criticism from Olympia's predominately white counterculture who would prefer "an event more in line with the community," presumably a Shakespeare or renaissance fair laden with papier maché. Contrary to this view, Lakefair is very much in line with the community. Compared to other events in Olympia, Lakefair draws far more people of color, young, working class and poor people. [21]

Lakefair brings an increase in homophobic harassment, leaving Olympia's queers feeling like they don't need the Gravitron or deep fried slime to feel unsettled. Many depart the county for the week in search of greener pastures.

Consistent praise comes for the "Demo-Burger" booth, the most popular food station at the Lakefair food court. An estimated twenty thousand burgers are flipped daily. To accomplish this amazing feat, Thurston County Democrats wrangle over 300 volunteers behind the counter and none of them have food handler's cards. For big-government-loving Democrats, the irony in this anarchism is a gift to fair goers, an opportunity to eat political contradiction while gambling with trichinosis and campylobacter.

---

20. For years, each July, during Lakefair, a spike in drunken mischief and a dip in local sales had shopkeepers wringing their hands and shaking their heads. Clumsy fairgoers, like bulls in china shops, had an upsetting effect on business. This prompted Lemon Days. Shops put out tables laden with bruised and broken merchandise. Were these items for sale or were they set out like this as an early warning system? There was free lemonade, yellow balloons and the faint smell of urine. These sales continue although some shops suffer less by closing for the wild week. **21.** *See* SOCIAL STUDIES, *third point.*

FOOD BANK / LOTT SEWAGE

Two of Olympia's most interesting institutions are best enjoyed back to back. The LOTT Sewage Center tour is the ideal follow-up to a volunteer shift at the Olympia Food Bank. After handling old bananas and beef ravioli, see where it all ends up. These two are just across the street from each other, a captivating before and after experience. Rich and poor, old and young, everyone's duty mixes in the collective soup flowing to Olympia's lowest elevation.

The sewage facility is called "LOTT." Why? No one knows. Maybe it's because Olympia makes A LOT of sewage? Or maybe it's because A LOT of time passed before anyone thought to establish the facility? Olympia had zero sewage treatment systems for the first hundred years of the city, and during that time A LOT of doo-doo got dumped in the bay.

Today, the system at LOTT remains the only one in the south sound to do advanced secondary nutrient removal. This is where billions of microbes have been employed (enslaved?) to break down nitrogen-based compounds.

Waste gas is distilled as surplus methane from a solid sludge digester and extracted as burnable gas from the H2S rich slop that's kept at a steady 95 degrees. In coarse terms, they're making fart juice from poop and it's put to work making heat, steam and electricity for the facility. How cool is that?

When an unexpected citywide dump run causes a methane overload, the surplus is ignited in electrified fire spires. Not only does this turn the toxic gas into water and carbon dioxide, it provides evening entertainment as fires of ignited passing gas light up the Olympia skyline.

An ocean of reclaimed water is pumped annually into lavender pipes for irrigation purposes. The system serves public parks and private landscaping as far away as the Tumwater Valley Golf Course.

The wastewater facility is on the same block as the Hands-On Children's Museum. It's not a museum about putting hands ON children. This is a museum FOR children where the children touch THINGS. Having a children's museum inches away from a sewage plant may be a bad idea.

ARTS WALK

Olympia may be off the grid of the art world, but it has made its own grid. Since the mid-90s, twice a year, downtown Olympia is turned into a community art space. Throngs of people mill through the streets and for a few hours, the town feels more vibrant and extroverted. Shops become music venues or galleries of visual art. The central downtown roads are closed to traffic and become busking spaces. Craft tables are set up in parking stalls. Buckets of sidewalk chalk are dispensed and the asphalt disappears into a rainbow of doodles.

There are occasional curious happenings that challenge the definition of art or go by without being called such. Strangers strike up deep conversations in the middle of intersections. Bits of yarn are tied to parking meters for no apparent reason. One time there was a guy who burned toast. Another year, the same guy demonstrated how to properly flatten empty soda cans with hammers. No one knows what happened to that guy.

Arts Walk is an over-stimulating cavalcade of beauty, creativity and genius. As the evening wears on, arts walkers acquire a glazed look, bumbling around in a fog. Over-saturated with inspiration, they stumble home to some calming ennui.

PROCESSION

Once a year, no matter who you are, for one hour, everyone puts aside their coolness and gets swept away by the magic, innocence and beauty of The Procession of The Species. It's a grand parade of costumed dancers, handmade puppets and sculpture depicting the natural realm, a celebration of art and environment. It includes life-sized whales, giraffes and other big game operated by hundreds of puppeteers, fluttering fabric simulating the sound, adorable children dressed as baby otters and old men dressed as shirtless gorillas going by in a psychedelic cavalcade that is just incredible.

There are three main rules: no live animals, no powered equipment and no words. This last rule includes the display of symbols such as a number, a crucifix or a swastika.

Procession has become an Olympia institution. There are regular characters known widely by their costumes.

There's a spinoff event, The Luminary, an after-dark pageant of see-thru animal lanterns.

Procession has had its share of dramas. A scandal broke out a few years ago over billing the city for thousands of dollars of reimbursements for items that were donated. A few years later, there was a man who dressed as Pan. Being a thing of Greek mythology and not an endangered species, this was considered a non-permitted entry. In the aftermath, emails from the event organizers surfaced that made it plain that it was his perceived sexual orientation that was the real issue. The year following this, there was a similar badly handled hullabaloo with a couple of mermaids.

As amazing as this organization is with papier mâché, they're not the greatest at managing finances or drama, their own or drama directed at them. Why should they? Procession is an unstoppable force of nature.

CAPITOL THEATER

From its beginning in 1924, the Capitol Theater has been used for a variety of purposes. In the 1930s, vaudeville was a regular occurrence on the stage. Some of the first films included a live music orchestra. At one point, the theater had two pipe organs and numerous concerts. In 1934, Judy Garland sang to a full house. In the 1950s, the theater was Olympia's G-rated movie venue. In 1980, the theater's owner and part-time organist, Andy Crow, prophesized that hippy oligarchs (previously overthrown by butt-rock oligarchs) would hold cinema culture hostage for the next thirty years. Sure enough, on September 1, 2010, the chains were broken and after decades of paying rent, The Olympia Film Society purchased the theater. OFS continues the tradition of the venue enjoying a variety of uses. Before going in, take a moment to notice the outside: circular stain glass windows depict the five stages of grief, a herd of Pegasiis and several dramatic masks are set into the façade.

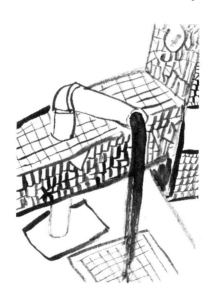

ARTESIAN WELL

Once upon a time, downtown Olympia had continuously flowing water fountains rising from its sidewalks. These were taps on the region's gigantic underground aquifer. People drank in good quantities. Then one day someone realized free water was discouraging sales of corn syrup energy drinks and booze.

The fountains were retired, dehydration spiked and soon there was only one fountain left, an angry pipe coming out of a parking stall. Threats of its closure prompted the formation of Friends Of The Well, a citizens group that kept city officials at bay by coordinating quarterly water testing. Eventually the city wrestled control away from The Friends by buying the land from the Diamond Parking Company and developed the lot as a "parklet."

When finished, an overindulgence of sugary art gave the site the appearance of the bedroom of a young girl. The city believed this would calm the boisterous street scene, but it had the opposite effect. The area became an urban terrarium for drive-by suburbanites gawking from SUVs slowing down just long enough to gasp. When inevitable vandalism tarnished the bright trimmings, there came a cliché broadcast of bourgeois indignation. The whole thing rolled out like a scene in a made-for-TV movie.

Turning an asphalt parking lot into an asphalt parklet seemed like a good idea to aloof planners, but it became a concentrated campground for Olympia's most scapegoated populations. Middle class rights advocates, feeling excluded, voiced outrage and demanded that the park be turned back into a parking lot or closed to the so-called vagrants.

Initially the city responded with posted hours, gates, additional lighting and daycare-inspired blacktop murals to give the pavement the appearance of grass and a winding brook, but when threats and assaults to city employees spiked, the park was fenced off.

Soon after, protesters broke in to add streamers and chalk drawings to the already saturated decor. Olympia police responded with pepper balls, tear gas, concussion grenades and arrests. The park remains closed, although the fence has been set to allow the thirsty people to fill water bottles at that same angry pipe, which continues to flow, providing free ice-cold spring water to people of a variety of backgrounds and circumstances.

FARMER'S MARKET

Not all that different from ones found in other towns, The Olympia Farmers Market is Olympia's main hub for locally raised produce. It's also something of a social parade. While conventional supermarkets offer fewer disruptions to the sacred practice of shopping, Olympia's farmer's market has a superior selection of fresh fruits, vegetables, meat, seafood and baked goods, most of which are from nearby.

I interviewed the owner of the market's often-overlooked, but long-standing and centrally located tie-dyed clothing booth. It's called Fossil Wear. The name is a reference to how very old hippies wear these outfits. However, younger people seem to be the larger part of the customers who flock to the piles of cotton clothing that has been crudely hand dyed. The success of the place is kind of a mystery. The owner has been in business for decades and can't account for it.

Local bands regularly play the outdoor grandstand. Local psychics offer drop-in readings. Local market executives enjoy entertaining scandals and embezzlement charges. Periodically, farmer vendors have been caught re-selling Costco produce.

SELF-CARE

Many people move to Olympia seeking spiritual sanctuary. Many have a desire to heal from past injuries, emotional and physical. Many find healing at one or more of the many places that offer it.

Others obtain a different kind of therapy by turning their noses up, making fun of it all and writing condescending letters to the editor, like this one:

> *Olympia is neck deep in the mental health quagmire, its parade of self-care clowns offer pampering affirmations and snake oil that only intensifies a perpetual inner crisis, keeping people shuttered in the political pacification of endless therapy...*

Wherever you sit on healing, therapy or self-care, there's no question that Olympia has a good number of resources, outlets, modalities and stores that offer recovery and recovery-related merchandise. Business seems to be booming. Depending on your needs and degree of mystical belief you may find what you're searching for at Radiance Herbs and Massage, Mystical Dreams Psychic Resource, Nalanda Healing Institute, Five Corners New Age Supply, Infrared Sauna & Energy Counseling, Psychic Sister, Tushita Kadampa Meditation Center, OlyYoga, Olyfloat, Gloryhouse Foursquare, The Bhanda Room, Al-Anon Olympia, Quality Self Storage, Olympia Free Clinic, Olympia Free Herbal Clinic, The Christian Science Reading Room, Euphorium Day Spa, and this is an incomplete list of the ever-changing alternative alternatives in downtown Olympia.

CHANGING SPACES

Olympia has a good history of things turning into other things. The former City of Olympia maintenance yard is now The Olympia Center. The former Olympia Center became The Olympian, then they moved to the small office building south of the former YMCA, then they moved to Tacoma. The school district took over the former Olympian and the former YMCA is rumored to be in transition as the next ACE Hotel.

The former Olympia post office on Capitol Way is now the offices of the Secretary of State. Olympia's post office before that, on the corner of Legion and Washington, is now home to a joke shop for high-class comedians. The former Kentucky Fried Chicken next to the 5th Avenue Dam is the office of the Applied Kinetics Company and the former Dairy Queen on Capitol Way is home to a group that sells electricity to farmers.

In 2006, the downtown Safeway supermarket became the Olympia City Hall. Five departments, previously spread across seven buildings, were now under one roof. To preserve a sense of local heritage, the city used the old Safeway ceiling arches to build the council dais and maintained the frozen foods section in the staff break room.

Olympia's most famous building transition happened on the afternoon of Friday, March 13, 1959 when fifteen boxcars slowly started rolling down the long gradual slope from Tumwater to Olympia. In the first ten minutes of the journey, the cars had only moved a few feet. No one noticed, but by the time the five o'clock whistle blew at the brewery, over 900 tons of freight cars were rolling fast, some reports said 25, but others said 30 or even 60 mph.

Regardless of the exact speed, in the end, what stopped the runaways was the Adams Street train station and most of the block around it. Kenneth Dilley, a 35 year-old telegraph operator, was killed instantly; his body was found a hundred feet from where he had been sitting.

In the months following the disaster, some called for rebuilding, but more said it didn't make sense and felt like trains were passé. The recently opened interstate still had its new car smell and the station sat in ruins for years.

The building was eventually repaired and became a sporting goods store and then a bike shop. Today, the former train station is a large dog food store for dogs both large and small.

There's no train service in Olympia. Residents board trains in Lacey. From downtown, it's a three-hour walk.

LACEY

Oliver Chester Lacey wasn't a nice guy. He had a reputation as a real estate opportunist and a cruel husband. Just before abandoning his disabled wife, he struck a deal with residents living north of Olympia and earned himself a modicum of immortality. In exchange for naming rights, Lacey agreed to carry the application for a new post office to Washington D.C. He travelled back east on foot, submitted the paperwork and was never heard from again.

While the area around that post office became known as Lacey, it was over seventy years later when Lacey became an official city. The forces at play around the city's incorporation shed light on the roots of ongoing Olympia-Lacey tensions.

In 1949, after a series of fires weren't reached in time by the Olympia fire department, residents around the Carpenter-Pacific intersection formed their own volunteer fire department. In 1953, after decades of travelling long distances to reach the Olympia schools, the same residents formed the North Thurston School District.

Frustrations nearly intensified into civil war in the 1960s when in a matter of months, the city of Olympia accelerated its northward expansion by making multiple annexations of newly re-zoned prime commercial areas. Olympia was trying to expand the range of its property tax jurisdiction by applying a State law that gave weighted voting power to the owners of commercial real estate over residential real estate.

Northern homeowners feared Olympia would soon swallow them up. They didn't want to be under the thumb of a government that didn't care about residential needs. They wanted to manage their own affairs. So, in 1966, in an effort to avoid becoming part of Olympia, the City of Lacey broke away.

Over the next five decades hostilities between the two cities only escalated. In the 1990s, t-shirts and bumper stickers with the slogan "LACEY SUCKS" became popular. Today, people in Olympia still complain about Lacey, calling it a retail wasteland. While there is some truth to this, the same is even more true about a lot of Olympia, and perhaps most striking, as of last year, Lacey has a greater percentage of its public land dedicated as parks.

WATER

Water is both Olympia's greatest cultural legacy and its greatest natural resource. An ocean of subterranean freshwater sits under the entire city.

These are the Olympia aquifers. Many are connected to naturally occurring artesian springs. [22]

Even before "It's the Water," became the motto of The Olympia Beer Company in 1902, brewers believed the secret to their excellent beer rested on the purity of region's outstanding artesian aquifers. For most of Olympia's history, beer was city's chief industry. Countless people and sometimes multiple generations worked their whole lives at the brewery. Despite the economic loss caused by the closing of the brewery in 2003, small breweries, distilleries and other beverage operations continue to hold Olympia water at the heart of their businesses. Today, the city owns the water rights to the brewery's old wells and has plans to tie these into its municipal water system. On October 8, 2018, the Tumwater fire department used 1.5 million gallons of it to douse the brewery's burning administration building, which in recent years had become a popular campground for homeless people.

Most of the city's municipal water supply draws from the aquifer at the remarkably productive wells located at the McAllister Wellfield facility located a few miles east of the city. Even when pumped out at a whopping eighteen thousand gallons per minute, McAllister's below ground sensors indicate no drop in the aquifer level. Last year the city served up over 2 billion gallons of water to customers.

While the overall volume and depth of the McAllister aquifers are unknown, the pumps draw from pipes that extend over 400 feet underground.

This depth explains why Olympia water quality tests much higher above national averages. Besides chlorination, there is no mineral removal or purification needed.

Similar purity is found at the public well in downtown. Despite nearly two centuries of industrial activity in the area, water quality tests continue to come back showing no toxins or contaminants leaching into the aquifer. A local folk legend has it that if you drink from the downtown artesian well, you'll never leave. If you choose to take this literally, the city recently installed a million dollar single stall toilet on the corner.

Water in Olympia takes on the wide variety of other forms: saltwater sound, estuary, creek, swamp, puddle, lake and river. Getting into it is a popular pastime. Some swim in the Puget Sound, but most say it's too polluted or cold. The closest lakes to downtown Olympia with public access are Ward and Munn. Ward offers more swimming room, but is more crowded at the boat launch. Munn is the opposite.

Along Henderson Way, just upstream of the Deschutes Bridge is a small parcel of private property that's open to anyone. It's a DIY playground for anti-government types who can't hack the hegemonies of nearby Pioneer Park. The owner, a lovable goon dressed like an old timey sailor, holds court in a plastic chaise lounge, occasionally barks like a thrombotic lifeguard and supervises two rope swings. One is ideal for children.

The other is ideal for spinal injury.

The Deschutes is semi-navigable and offers seasonal inner tube passage. On hot weekends, it's a parade of beer guzzling watery mayhem. The Black River is further away, has a slower current and is better for canoes and kayaks. The nearest legal quarry to swim in is at the Tenino sandstone quarry. You can ride the CWT bikeway there. There's an illegal quarry, everyone knows where it is (everyone except me).

There are municipally sanctioned life guarded swimming areas at Long, Black and Deep Lakes. There are dozens of other lakes in Olympia that are dangerously private.

Lake Cushman is a large manmade lake that can be reached by car in less than an hour. Beware bad energy related to the lake having displaced a Native community and it being named after one of Isaac Stevens' thugs.

Boating as transportation still occurs in Olympia. During rush hour, cross-inlet canoe and kayak traffic can get heavy enough that paddlers may see one another.

A few miles north of downtown Olympia is an island that's a public park. This is Hope Island, the southernmost stop along the Cascadia Marine Trail, a 140-mile saltwater paddler highway that starts at the Canadian border. Poison ivy plants outnumber tent sites 10,000 to 1, so be sure to bring your Tecnu and make a reservation for camping. Hope is only accessible by boat, but if you don't have a boat, at low tide it's less than a quarter mile swim from Carlyon Beach off Steamboat Island Road.

If you enjoy eating food that is the color and texture of flu season phlegm, visit the island during clamming and oyster season (May). You'll find horse clams, butter clams, manila clams, littlenecks, piddocks, oysters, geoducks and beached jellyfish in good numbers.

---

22. An artesian well is a spring that flows on its own pressure, without needing a pump.

GARBAGE

At 500 tons of solid waste per day, Olympia is about even with national averages, but local trash doesn't linger long. It can't. Twenty years ago, Olympia overwhelmed its Hawks Prairie landfill and held a ceremonial closing of the historic dump with the somber burial of its last bag of trash. Today, the city's garbage is sealed away in trucks and trains and shipped off to the gigantic garbage vault outside of Roosevelt, Washington. If these garbage exports were to stop, the region would qualify for Federal disaster relief in just seven days. (The Hawks Prairie Garbage Center offers tours peppered with crushing environmental statistics like this one.)

HARBOR HOUSE

The City of Olympia's "Harbor House" is a beautiful glass, metal and wood structure perched on Percival Landing. The architecture is an homage to the historic buildings that once lined the bay. The small house is ideal for a group of 3 or 4 people. You can rent it for $39/hour or $1.09/minute. The house is locked, empty and surrounded by homeless people.

INTERSTATE FIVE

I-5 is the only continuous highway to connect the three nations of North America. It's the primary transportation artery of the west coast and it passes through Olympia. In Tumwater, the Interstate passes in a carnal sense. In 1952, local officials surrendered downtown Tumwater by offering it up for sacrifice. Its corpse was buried under millions of tons of concrete and asphalt. Today, between exits 103 and 104, motorists are quite literally passing over Tumwater's historic core.

The Interstate had an enormous effect on every town and city along its path, and Olympia is no exception. Before 1956, travelers had to pass through downtown Olympia on their way to Seattle, Portland, Spokane, Hood Canal, the peninsula and the coast. Local business was tied to this traffic. The loss of this traffic created a vacuum that effectively killed downtown business. Today older residents wax nostalgic and grieve this loss. However, a different kind of downtown rose from the ashes of the old one. In the vacated stores, eclectic small businesses, odd shops and unusual restaurants continue to thrive in the space made by the absence of big stores and high-volume traffic.

NETTLES

Lauded as a cure-all by devotees and celebrated at an annual festival at Calliope Farm, the nettle is the official urtica of the city of Olympia. Is there any better way to celebrate the coming of spring than flogging one's rear end with a bouquet of thorny plants? Veteran enthusiasts go further and sanctify their vernal stir by chugging fluids made from concentrated horseradish kim chi and spend the rest of the day wearing nothing but horseflies.

MOUNT RAINIER

Hidden most of the time by clouds and tall trees, it's not unusual to be stopped in ones tracks when "the mountain comes out." Mount Rainier, named for Pete Rainier (who never set foot in Washington, let alone glimpsed his mountain from afar), is the perfect distance from Olympia— close enough to offer a view, but far enough away that Olympia shouldn't suffer too badly when it explodes. Mount Rainier has a history of destructive eruptions that occur at regular intervals. Presently it's late for the next one and is considered one of the most dangerous volcanoes in the world.

Sometimes when people want to visit Mt. Rainier, they accidentally go to Rainier, Washington. This small town near Olympia was named for its purportedly breathtaking view of the mountain. The naming occurred before a lot of people had gotten any closer. Today, even residents of Rainier admit that there are countless other towns with objectively superior views.

As if being inappropriately named wasn't bad enough, Rainier the town has a very unlucky history. Between 1920 and 1930 all the businesses burned down in dozens of unrelated non-arson fires. Local business owners either went bust, got superstitious or took the hint. The town nearly dissolved into oblivion. Today the heart of town is marked by a vintage era laundromat.

SALMON

Starting in late August or early September, countless giant salmon choreograph Marine World quality performances between the 4th and

5th Avenue Bridges. The fish aren't trying to impress anyone, they're just trying to transition from saltwater to fresh, climb the salmon ladder that passes under the Capitol Lake dam and make it to their spawning grounds. The aquatic capers are augmented by the exhilarations of hungry seals and the gasping crowds that gather on the viewing platform. Salmon Stewards are 100% human volunteers from The Olympia Stream Team who keep regular hours on the platform to answer questions about salmon migration. Local fascination with salmon ties to a time when these migrations were a key part of local life.

WESTSIDE

Even by local standards, the westside is a balinaged jantricized place, a bipolar mix of easy-breezy folk life, blended with terrifying conspiracy-rich hippie paranoia.

Cheerful vegans can suddenly run hungry for meat; wolf anarchists can blossom with unexpected warmth; red-blooded Greeners can call 9-1-1 for a flower. Behind every smile seething leftist anger is waiting to be triggered by the slightest slight. Behind every atomic hostility, a grim grimace is stilting over a soft core.

Love the Olympia westside. Don't try to figure it out. This is where Twilight meets the Twilight Zone. It's five hundred acres riddled with contradiction.

The westside has a dark history of animal-on-animal violence. Keep an eye on your pets and bare legs. Cat hunting raccoon gangs and irate possums can strike when you least expect it.

If you're feeling harried, escape to the quiet of a back alley in this densely laid shire. You'll find bucolic backyard farmlets and the tiniest tiny houses surrounded by miniature chickens.

For the most part, the westside is held in the rainbow grip of a Phish and chips mafia, but it has pockets held by other saints of resistance, alternatives to the alternative alternatives worth alternating to. There's a guilty pleasure zone, the forbidden Capital Mall. The only thing special about it is that it's nothing special. This is where Olympia's mainstream masses seek sanctuary from westside lefties.

At The Westside Lanes, six decades of unambiguous tobacco gas and spotty ventilation make it a nicotine time machine. From your first breath to last, you'll be brought to a smokier era.

The aisles of the westside Grocery Outlet are gravid with candied rage, smashing shopping carts, bulging biceps, unrestricted mothers strolling with miniature monkeys clamped like barrettes to purse straps and burlesque ex-boyfriends lurching with frozen food frozen to their manes. This is also a place of generosity and true love.

Capital Cho at 2419 Harrison has been Olympia's unofficial Asian cultural center for thirty years. The owner, Kim Chi explained to me that "Cho" is a Vietnamese word that means market. Kim chi (the food) is also one of the top sellers. The store primarily stocks Chinese, Thai and Vietnamese foods, but there are Japanese, Filipino and Korean items. The walk-in freezer is home to a good variety of frozen mysteries from the deep. Some of the coolest things they sell include jackfruit, durian, "Thai spinach" and an amazing tool for splitting it lengthwise. They also have popsicles sold individually made from hornet honey and kidney beans.

Approach the Westside like a cultural study; keep your feet rooted (or rotted) in reality. You'll come away with stories to shock and delight your grandkids.

THE CO-OP

At the heart of the westside is a cult posing as a health food store called the Olympia Food Cooperative. It opened in 1977 at around 8 a.m. and by noon that same day, its companion shop, The Free Store, opened.

Today, The Free Store continues to outpace the volume of its not-free sponsor store. As its name suggests, the price of any item at The Free Store is the effort of removal. This is the largest free resource exchange in Western Washington and people flock to it like fake snow. In this college town rich with rich short-term young adults, The Free Store enjoys an influx of toasters, microwaves and food processors at the tail end of each academic quarter. Some claim the Free Store allows a life free from money. This kind of eco-boasting is not uncommon, but dubious.

Don't get so laden with free paraphernalia, that you forget to visit the Co-op. Quasi-paid volunteer workers are compensated by a store credit on twenty-five percent of one hundred and twelve dollars of non-taxable purchases for every seven and five quarters percent of an hour worked multiplied by an aggregate daily sales coefficient and adjusted by variable task variables. Customers may purchase rotten fruit for thirty-five cents per pound from a compost coffin under the produce shelf. There's a local snake oil section that has unguents made from fuzz, dust and chaff.

The Co-op does more business than a Costco and is hilariously undersized. At off-peak times it feels crowded; during busy times the store feels like a disaster area food riot. They sell everything from toilet paper to broccoli milk, but they don't sell Coke or Palestinian ice cream cones. There are also bans on items from China, so there are no Chinese made things at all. This includes the store's electronics and explains the twig abacus that is used instead of a cash register.

For a less romantic shopping experience, try the newer Eastside location where a food buffet and proximity to Lacey has a desexualizing effect.

RAMTHA

Olympia's many cults have capitalized on the region's inordinate number of lonely people willing to trade critical thinking for a sense of belonging. Olympia's most beloved cult is located inside a turreted compound girded by energy absorbing copper clad cairns.

Thousands of seemingly rational, high-functioning Olympia residents pay a tithe to Lord Ramtha and attend mandatory semi-annual 8-day blindfolded art therapy inductions that culminate with the principal deity dropping down from a crystal chamber to gibber nonsense in a falsetto that sounds like an intoxicated Katherine Hepburn doing an impersonation of a modern citizen of India.

The Ramtha origin story has several versions, but the broad strokes involve Judy Hampton (a high school homecoming queen who divorced the Marlboro man) getting knocked dead by a frozen grapefruit then rising up hours later as Judith Zebra Knight enchanted channel to his holiness, Master Teacher Lord Ronald R.R. Ramtha, living ghost of the thirty thousand year old King of Lemuria. [23]

There are questions Knight/Ramtha has been asked publicly. Like, why does the ghost speak in English and not whatever was the language of Lemuria? Only the most vague answers have been supplied and when Carl Sagan led an effort to audit Ramtha, he concluded that the dogma was "a series of banal homilies." [24]

Gaps between science and Ramtha are patched up with magical thinking, allowing a buffer for leaders and members to fabricate reality to suit their needs.

If you have doubts, it's likely that you're just not living a remarkable life, nor ready to ride the white spider into this torsion cavalcade of Zebra's zany zeal.

---

23. Lemuria is an imaginary world, like Atlantis, Narnia, Neverland, etc. **24.** Carl Sagan's audit of The Ramtha School of Enlightenment: positiveatheism.org/writ/saganbur.html

PRIEST POINT

Priest Point Park has been renamed Squaxin Park, but the pointy point of Olympia's largest park is still called Priest. Pointedly, the land was purchased by the city in 1905. Before that, it had been the site of a Catholic mission run by Oblate monks where Squaxin natives were invited (i.e. coerced) to work (i.e. accept Jesus) on their farm (i.e. brainwashery).

During World War II there were several canons installed at Priest Point to defend the city in the event of a Japanese invasion. The city retains the canons as part of its municipal arsenal at a storage facility near Steilacoom.

In the early years of the park, there was a primitive zoo built and managed by teenage zookeepers. It was a simple menagerie of wooden pens that housed locally trapped deer, goats, raccoons, possums, squirrels, seagulls, crows, red-breasted robins and a family of harbor rats.

Letters in The Olympian about the needless cruelty of the zoo start piling up as early as 1916. The final chapter of Olympia's zoo story is riddled with unsubstantiated rumors. The straw that broke the camel's back was the arrival of a large bear. In the end, all of the animals, including the bear, escaped or were killed when the zoo caught fire or was burned by activists in the mid-1950s. No one at the city could say what really happened, but parks staff suggested that it seems like a thing that would have been brushed under the rug.

The remains of the zoo were quickly cleared and in its place, a small wooden building was built for an ice cream stand. Only three years passed before this also burned down. It was replaced by an unburnable children's wading pool, however in 1996 this was demolished by jackhammers.

Today, the former zoo/ice cream/pool site near where Olympia's outdoor summer Shakespeare festival occurs. The troupe that puts on the plays calls themselves "Animal Fire Productions" as a memorial to what happened over ninety years ago.

ASSORTED OTHER PARKS

There was a period when all that Harry Fains Park had was a single seesaw. Today, with the addition of expanded playground equipment, there has been a gain, but also a kind of loss. The single seesaw had a minimalist elegance.

Burfoot Park got its name from the Burfoot Family who used to own the property. The family had shoes and didn't have problems stepping on thistles, thorns or burrs of any kind. Each year a handful of visitors leave the park without severe rashes due to contact with forest plants. The central meadow is a good site for Capture The Flag.

In 1961, G-rated movie theater owner Art Zabel purchased a small hazelnut orchard near San Francisco Street. Over the next decade he converted the property into a 3-acre rhododendron gallery with common and rare specimens of the Washington State flower. In 2015 the property was acquired by the city and continues to draw thousands of state flower buffs.

In 1926, the Chehalis Western Railroad Company laid a path for what is today Olympia's 23-mile north-south bicycle mega-highway. At the north end of the CWT is Woodard Bay, an 870-acre wilderness preserve that boasts the state record for most blue heron rookeries. There are also a lot of bats. At the south end of the CWT, one can connect with another former railroad turned bike path. The 14-mile Tenino-Yelm Railway was first built in 1869, one of the earliest in the state.

The letters of LBA Park stand for Little Baseball Association, an Olympia-based baseball arranger. Contrary to a common misunderstanding, the "little" in their name refers to youth, not size. The Olympia LBA has nothing to do with Eddie Gaedel or collectible baseball figurines. LBA is a medium-sized group that donated the large piece of land in 1974.

There was a controversy over logging the forests bordering LBA Park to make way for a densely laid mini-mansion townhouse development. Opponents of the logging plan were frustrated that the name of the park didn't inspire more sympathy and spent time explaining that the park has nothing to do with Lyndon B. Johnson. Forest advocates begged the city long enough that eventually the city shelled out $5 million and bought the 74 acres from the developer.

Watershed Park was also once slated to be clear-cut and in 1955 the issue went all the way to the State Supreme Court. These 150 acres were home to Olympia's first municipal waterworks. Nineteenth century rusted ruins are still visible among the skunk cabbage and big leaf maples.

West Central Park also began after neighborhood opposition to commercial development and one wealthy resident (unwilling to let the fourth corner of Harrison and Division fall to an ever-expanding retail wasteland) bought the corner parcel outright. It was declared a privately-owned public park. Today, it's not clear what is being accomplished, but things seem to be happening. Cement road barricades have been painted to look like bricks. An information kiosk shows plans that include gazebos, enhanced landscaping and covered eating areas. If you love automobile noise and air pollution, this might be the perfect picnic site for you.

Several times a year, during peak rainfall

(September to May), Yauger Park changes its unofficial name to Yauger Lake. At these times, lovers can take a romantic canoe trip across nine baseball diamonds submerged under five feet of storm discharge to a timer switch located in the middle of the lake, flip on a hundred high-watt halogens and enjoy an electric summer in February.

In the 1980s, Grass Lake Park was purchased by the city in a marathon political battle involving city staff, neighborhood groups, developers and certain city council members. The story of how it all went down got so dense that I lost consciousness. Continuing in that vein, the wildlife sanctuary comes with a 211-page user guide. (Download a free copy of this epic 15MB page-turner from the city website: olympiawa.gov/city-services/parks/parks-and-trails/grass-lake-nature-park)

A greenbelt mini-jungle called the Garfield Nature Trail is home to a very strange thing. About halfway down the path, about halfway up the tree line, nature enthusiasts and bird watchers pass under a suspended sewer. It's suspended on wooden stilts in the trees. During the peak bath and shower hours, this greenish pipe drips greenish wastewater. Aside from the odd sewer line up in the trees, the tiny jungle offers a Zen space, a break from the hustle and bustle and is a predominantly pleasant pedestrian short-cut.

The Garfield Nature Trail ends at the mouth of one of Olympia's ugliest parks. What West Bay Park lacks in appearance, it makes up for in views.

This is a good place to appreciate Mount Rainier, Budd Inlet, the port and the downtown skyline. This used to be a waterfront industrial area and a sawmill. The Rotarians had a role in the concrete esplanade. The cement is pre-defaced with the embossed names of some famous ones. Who cares?

Let's get out of this former industrial wasteland and make our way south following the old train tracks to an actual one.

MOTTMAN INDUSTRIAL PARK

One of the best ways to get to know Olympia is to spend time at Mottman. Here you'll find thousands of blue-collar late-night clock zombies in dozens of medium-sized factories making all manner of materialisimo. Many of these plants operate two or more shifts, which keeps the area humming around the clock. There are hundreds of places like this all over the country, but in Olympia there's a special factory that squirts out corrugated black plastic drainage pipes, another one blows spinning molten polyethylene cylinders into 1 and 2-liter soda bottles, there's a plant that makes steel cranes and one that makes fake bricks. The author of this book has been employed at most of these. Mottman is home to the state's largest dog food-processing plant. The author never worked there.

DESCHUTES FALLS PARK

One of Olympia's newest parks is so far away that you might want to bring a passport just in case. Or, you might want to not go at all. The hour-long nauseating drive winds you through the heart of manure country.

If you're only a little carsick when you get there, just step into the park's single port-o-potty. It's perched on a slope. It also wobbles. It's written in faded ink that the unit was last cleaned when the park opened in 2017. I couldn't tell if I was getting light-headed from the smell or from the angle of the rocking floor. Luckily, someone stapled a pink purse strap next to the toilet; holding onto it reduced my vertigo.

If you haven't died in the toilet, don't expect much in that regard from these so-called falls. Thrill seeking cliff jumpers should bring a ladder and a kiddie pool. I've had more fun leaping off cinder blocks. As for water, the barely moving liquid, in what's more drainage ditch than river, smells like number one and in some places resembles bug-choked correction fluid. The only recreation I saw happening were screaming teenagers flapping wildly at swarms of angry black flies, yellow jackets and the unnaturally large mosquitos.

Deschutes Falls Park has zero garbage cans, so it's on track to become an open pit landfill. It does have a good collection of broken glass, graffiti and rain-damaged erotica. Outside the door of the rusting trailer of the on-site caretaker is a framed diploma from a machete convalescence program.

There's no cell service. It's a half hour before you'll be back to one bar. Short term you'll have to share your complaints with the other idiots who fell for this recreation trap.

HOLY SH*T PARK

In 2019, Olympia's long-time commercial mushroom factory moved to the middle of the state far away from sensitive noses. I removed this chapter, then received reasonable complaints. This is after all a history book. So, I've brought this one back, to be part of the record.

In 1967, upcoming mushroom-magnate Cameron Ostram bought a small farm on the edge of town on the corner of Steilacoom and Marvin. At the time, the only thing out there besides the farm was the dump. As the Olympia metropolitan area spread north, "mushroom corner," as it became known, stopped being the middle of nowhere.

The area was soon awash in box stores, schools, offices and homes. Ostrom's remained a family-owned business, but had grown into the largest mushroom plant in Washington (or Oregon), employing 300 people and producing forty thousand pounds of mushrooms daily.

How does one grow mushrooms on this scale? What agricultural magic is required?

The process is simple. You take chicken manure, lots and lots of chicken manure. More chicken manure than you want to be imagining right now.

It gets worse.

It all gets loaded into a shallow swimming pool that works like a crock-pot and slow-cooks the feces for a week. And, high-yield mushroom production is continuous. A fresh crock of shit must be started up several times a day. The atmospheric byproduct is beyond belief. The amplified aroma is on an unprecedented industrial scale.

(What I'm about to tell you next is such a doozy that it's hard for me to hold steady while writing. It seems like the stuff of the strangest nightmare.)

As Ostrom's was freshening the air with weaponized manure stink, just across the street, there is a place called The Regional Athletic Complex (RAC).

Developed in 2009, the RAC is a campus of baseball diamonds and soccer fields. On a typical evening or weekend THERE WERE BACK-TO-BACK GAMES.

HUNDREDS OF FAMILIES WOULD BE SITTING IN BLEACHERS, SITTING ON THE GRASS, OR ON BLANKETS. HAVING PICNICS, EATING SNACKS OR EVEN EATING DINNER AND OCCASIONALLY CHEERING FOR THEIR CHILDREN AND THEIR CHILDREN WERE PLAYING BASEBALL, PLAYING SOCCER, SWEATING, RUNNING, BREATHING…

--{{{ BREATHING HARD }}}--

But, the air.

They were breathing the air.

It was surreal.

I spoke with dozens of residents who lived in recently built homes in the sprawling neighborhoods around the RAC. I asked them nicely how they could buy a home here. Not one of them thought it was weird. They said they barely notice "it" anymore.

How was this possible?

This wasn't standard caliber farm odor. This was the off-gas from countless simmering high-tech high-volume gigantic doo-doo slurry cookers.

For decades, there was an unspoken agreement to not mention IT. When pressed, I heard repeat comments about new technologies at the plant or how it was getting better, but none of that was ever true. Ostrom's production numbers only doubled over their last few years. Their patented slow-cook manure heating process allowed for expansion, and more expansion. Never in human history had feces been cooked in these quantities. At such a proximity to a population center it was incredible. At such proximity to a modern outdoor recreation complex, it just seemed cruel.

That said, putting aside my squeamishness, all of this was harmless. Ostrom's was following latest Department of Ecology standards. It's better to recycle poop in this manner than throw it in a river, right? They were here before the houses, let alone before the stores, right? Ostrom's didn't decide to locate the RAC here, right? The plant employs a lot of people. Mushrooms are a healthy food. So...

But, come on.

The smell? Seriously?

Sadly, now you'll have to just take my word for it, or you can visit their new site appropriately located next to the Hanford nuclear waste disposal center.

WOLF HAVEN

As human civilization spreads ever further towards total global domination, all living things are feeling a mounting strain. It's not easy being a wild animal. This is particularly true for wolves. Of course Olympia, undying defender of underdogs, is home to one of the world's largest wolf sanctuaries.

Since 1982, Wolf Haven has provided a home for over 200 wolves, 3 foxes, 6 coyotes and even a handful of hybrid wolf-dogs. Facility tours include exchanging heartbreaking glances with the beautiful beasts that are held here for their protection and ours behind cyclone fencing. Signs written in wolf are posted to remind the caged canines that humanity is profoundly sorry, and that for now this is the best we can do. Hang in there.

Through education and lobbying for the expansion and maintenance of protected wilderness areas, Wolf Haven is a leader in wolf advocacy. Only a few miles down the road is one of the area's largest pig farms, which offers a weird, but iconic follow up tour.

BLACK HOUSES

Duane Moore practices dentistry in the next town over. In Olympia, he owns a vintage morgue-themed bar on Fourth Avenue and more than a dozen residential properties, which includes the historic Track House. Duane's houses are visually striking. Each one has been completely painted flat black.

The surrounding lawns are kept meticulously wild.
You don't need to be a Catholic priest to the see the
obvious.

Duane is in league with the devil, and this is true
as long as you believe that the devil is the Thurston
County assessor. The black paint and the scruffy
grasses have a calming effect on Duane's property
taxes.

You don't need to pin thumbtacks to a map to see
that Duane's houses are forming no pattern
whatsoever, or as everyone in Olympia will tell you,
a pentagram. You don't need to read The Inferno
backwards to know that once this nonexistent
upside-down star is complete, a gateway to Hell will
open up, allowing passage of a convoy of
unchristian superpower that will set fire to St.
Martin's University and install Duane on a charcoal
throne as king of its smoldering ruins.

Duane is thriving on reduced property valuations
and vague associations. His low-lit bar has a stone
autopsy table. He rides around town in a goat drawn
chariot and sleeps in a coffin made of human teeth.

ANCIENT AIRPORT

The Olympia airport is so disused that some of
the gates are made of driftwood and beer bottles.
This isn't a problem. There aren't commercial
flights anymore. The only things passing in or out
are private and cargo planes, and tons of safety

information cards. The world's largest producer of word-free seat pocket hieroglyphics is located near the old airport. Drawing on Olympia's inordinate number of visual artists, Interactive Research has been banging out crash cards for 46 years. Next time you're bored on a flight look for MADE IN OLYMPIA at the bottom of the card.

COMPOST CITY

Olympia has won awards for its municipal compost collection program and is considered among the most compost-friendly cities in the United States. A list of the wide-ranging accepted biodegradable compostable items has been set to a delightful jingle with an intoxicating beat. The lyrics include:

"onion skins, carrot tops, corn husks and cobs / nut shells, egg shells, pizza crusts and pits / chicken bones, beef, ham bones and turkey / veal, venison, goose, lamb and goat / calcareous detritus, shrimp, prawn and squid / crawdad, geoduck, lobster claws and tails / cat bones, dog bones, canary, and parrot / hamster, gerbil, guinea pig and mouse / bear, cougar, mountain goat and moose / antlers, hooves, fangs, horns and claws / talons, whiskers, furs, pelts and paws / chest hair, back hair, leg, arm and neck hair / armpit, pubic, foot, nose and hand / nails from your finger, lower lip and toe / deer ticks, stink bugs,

stick bugs and moths / praying manti, Egyptian dung beetles / locusts, roaches, ants, fleas and flies / skunks, squirrels, possums, raccoons, chipmunks mice, boars and voles / starfish, barnacles, seaweed and gulls / amniotic fluid, before and afterbirths / livers, hearts, lungs and marrow / stem cells, kidney stones, tonsils and pearls / old teeth, baby teeth, scabs and blisters / dandruff, blood, phlegm, pee and puss / uteri, scroti, ovaries and balls / fallopian tubes, vas deferens and what? unclaimed corpses, pies, eyes and milk."

For the complete list of things one
can compost in Olympia visit:

www.olympiawa.gov

HALLOWEEN

Some say that everyday is Halloween in Olympia. However, you can only get free candy on October 31. Prime yields of sweets are reaped at a development on the Westside called Cedrona.

The south capital neighborhood has the best haunted houses and elaborate jack-o-lantern carvings, but the governor's mansion is a total time-waster. The long line and a security search only leads to a photo op and a hand sanitizer dampened granola bar.

GRIM(M)

Founded in 1945, Grimm Collections Incorporated is the longest-running debt retirement firm in southwest Washington. They were the first company to have a drive-up window. Today, "using a unique blend of advanced technology, proven techniques and a highly trained staff of seasoned collection professionals, Grimm has a solid track record" (of squeezing money out of poor people).

When I interviewed the owners, no one besides me thought their name was funny. They pointed out that the family name has an extra M. They put a lot of emphasis in shifting the focus to the services they provide their creditor clients, not the grim nature of blood-letting and shakedowns.

AUTO MALL

The Olympia Auto Mall is the largest car sales conglomerate in Washington State. This is deep in mainstream muggledom, about as far from the counterculture as one can get. If you approach from its rear end via one of several enchanting pedestrian paths, you will travel from thinning suburban developments into the forest, then there's an abruptness to the change in the scenery. The woods are replaced with crisp lines of precise dealership landscapism. It feels like you just passed into anti-Narnia

Afraid of the dark? Can't stand stars? The Auto Mall has light pollution so thick, you can spread out a towel, sip iced-tea and work on your tan at 3 a.m.

TUMWATER HILL

Overlooking Olympia, perched on Tumwater Hill is a small elementary school with a mysterious tower on its south side.

The story of the tower goes back to 1987 when the south side of the hill was clear-cut. The loggers agreed if they could clear-cut it, the land would be forever after used for a nature trail. At the time, on a fair day, from up in the tower, one could see all the way to Centralia.

Today, the nature trail is in full bloom, trees have grown and there's simply no view to view from the viewing tower. Even from its highest point, as you look out, one's face is faced with view-blocking trees, there's nothing but bark for as far as the eye can see.

Newcomers unaware of the history have theorized on the purpose of the strange tower ranging from student isolation discipline, a prop for Romeo and Juliet and a gravity demonstration device.

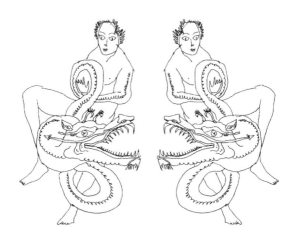

BALLOON ARTIST

For twenty years, Gene Bowdish has been making balloon animals in Olympia. Gene's long-winded musings on economics and social science are confusing. It's not clear if that's a result of his disability or part of his shtick. During our interview, he acknowledged that his path is an unusual one and his "economic model," as he calls it, relies on people "feeling sympathy." Almost everyone enjoys his balloons and gives him a dollar or two for a dog, bird or sword.

Gene sometimes gets harassed or accused of running a scam. He offers haters smaller balloons for free and hands everyone little squares of paper advertising his web site. The site reads like a Dr. Bronner's label with advice on how his discoveries, mathematical formulas and economic analysis can be applied to cancer therapy. There are optical illusions and connect the dot activities. There are parts of the site that don't make sense, but it's clear that Gene makes lemonade as best he can from the lemons he's been given. Olympia is lucky to have him around.

MIMA MOUNDS

The Mima Mounds are regular humps of dirt dimpling the prairies a few miles south of Olympia that may have formed hundreds or thousands of years ago. Today they are part of a national landmark. A visit offers stunning views of miniature hills rolling out as far as the eye can see. Most of the mounds are only about ten feet across and four feet high.

A recent study gave new support to what had long been considered among the wilder and less likely hypotheses, that gophers made them. The 2013 study used a sped up computer model to show the effects of tunneling rodents over hundreds of years. Other origin studies of equal credibility have looked at the effect of wind-blown debris trapped in low shrubs, shrinkage and swelling of clay in the soil and the effect of seismic waves bouncing through the unique soil composition of Olympia's prairies.

There are more than a few wilder theories. One involves a lost tribe of Native Americans who built the mounds as templates for a fish net making operation. There's a theory concerning a meandering stream of saltwater, the exodus of an artificial tsunami triggered by landscape artist space aliens. Another claims the mounds are the abandoned shelters of prehistoric goat-sized ants.

My favorite theory concerns an ice-age era group of blue skinned mystics who descended from their northern frozen wilderness to maintain the mounds as earth sculpture calendars. I'm also fond of the theory that the mounds were mashed into the ground by the hooves of mastodons as premating mammoth masturbation mumps. There are a few hundred other theories, which leads me to suggest my own: that the true purpose of the Mima Mounds is to spark the imagination.

Regardless of what force or combination of forces you believe created Olympia's Mima Mounds, it's a beautiful place to visit and during the spring, the wildflowers and rare butterflies are inspiring.

MONARCHISTS

Olympia is the only U.S. city under a monarchy system. [25] The Queen of Lacey, Olympia, Tumwater and greater Thurston County is called The Lakefair Queen. She is crowned annually with a tiara of glass, rules for eleven months before being paraded on the back of a convertible and shot out of a cannon. This ties to a tradition dating back to the last ice age when primitive European societies elected a young maiden and fed her to a dinosaur.

---

25. In 1982, Olympia voters stripped the mayor position of executive authority. Since then, the mayor has been a title-only position. Aside from ribbon cuttings and handing Macklemore a key to the city, the mayor is effectively nothing more than another member of the City Council. The person with the real power is the person who runs the city, The City Manager.

ANARCHISTS

I want to say something about the people in Olympia who identify as anarchists.

FIREWORKS

In the early 1960s, Olympia, Lacey and Tumwater agreed on a fireworks compromise.[28] Lacey has the night BEFORE Independence Day. Tumwater has rights to the actual holiday and Olympia was banned from municipal fireworks discharge within ten days of the Fourth. This is why Olympia always has its fireworks on the third Sunday in July. [29]

---

28. It's only a rumor that there was a period of near-constant fireworks-related unrest where everything from the smallest bottle rockets to military-grade cannon ordinance were launched across city borders. The situation never flared up, the governor never threatened to call in the National Guard and no Hollywood celebrities showed up to help broker a settlement. The whole arrangement was worked out peacefully. No fireworks were shot into city council chambers or any other public buildings. **29.** If you absolutely must see municipal fireworks on the 4th of July, then you'll have to go to Tumwater. You definitely want to bike or walk there or else you'll never get home. A single lane bridge is the only way out of the gigantic parking area.

FAR WESTSIDE

A gradual drift draws many towards an indefinable realm called The Far Westside. Its boundary is moving, a greying grey of overcast opinions, where suburbia ends and the forest begins, the area between Evergreen and Shelton, a place increasingly enriched with alternatives.

Many end up here but then drift even further, all the way to the sea and then float away into the misty mysteries. The Far Westside is home to those who live among rusting busses parked under jungle canopies and tarpaulin, eat ferns and drink mountain milk.

BORDEAUX

Out in Capital Forest, a dozen or so miles from Olympia, there's a long-abandoned logging town, a graveyard of concrete hips and iron ribs overgrown with vines and trees. This is all that remains of the hospital, post office, school, church and other buildings. It's the perfect site for filming a dystopian movie or having a weird picnic.

Climbing among the ruins, towers and numerous cement pyramids along the little river, one can only guess at the industry that occurred here over a hundred years ago when this was one of the largest cities in Thurston County.

Today, Bordeaux has a population of zero.

Courtney Love owned Bordeaux for a number of years. There's some rumor over this being one of the places where Kurt Cobain's ashes were scattered. Some sources say there were several places, including Scatter Creek, McLain Creek, Aberdeen's Wishkah River, The Namgyal Monastery in Ithaca and some other undisclosed locations.

SLEATER KINNEY

Sleater had a farm south of present day Lacey. Kinney had one several miles to the north. At the time, there wasn't a road connecting their farms to Pacific Avenue, which at the time was the main highway to Seattle and Portland. These guys weren't the type of farmers who waited around for government handouts. So, in order to get their produce to market, they paved their own road connecting the two farms and named the street after one of Olympia's most famous bands.

CLIMATE

Olympia's generally wet climate has an effect on the natural environment, the people and their things. The forest and its inhabitants seem to love it. Many human residents claim to love it too. The high humidity makes the air very nice to breathe, but the effect on books and printed documents can be frustrating. Mold, fungus, mildew and rot are some of Olympia's top natural resources. Aside from its effect on paper, the winter darkness coupled with long runs of wet weather, makes Olympia a writer's paradise.

CONCLUSION

I hope these rough illustrations of this partially invisible city have piqued your curiosity and you'll study the deeper levels, separate the sound ballet of Olympia's saltwater from the breakdance of its clouds.

As your understanding of Olympia continues, as the place starts to make more sense, you may notice your hands falling on all manner of unlikely opportunities; you may find yourself pulled into all sorts of life-changing experiences (selling twigs, writing books).

This city may never crack a donkey or bust a mule, but it does crackle static pajamas in its dry hampers. Packed with tricky tactile tractates and contrary to a popular misconception, many of Olympia's residents experience disappointment and a handful haven't had a massage this week.

Olympia rides six white horses. Olympia comes around its own mountain. This is a city of departures. Each spring, fresh batches of Evergreen graduates join the upstream transition into the dematriculated residential counterculture where they typically stay for two years. This explains the disproportionate number of twenty-three year olds with one eye on an I-5 on-ramp. Perhaps a vestige from stagecoach times, exiting InterCity bus passengers regularly offer drivers a fond farewell.

Olympia is the dead end of the Puget Sound,
the furthest point from the open sea.
A great deal collects at the bottom
of this great drain.

This may include you.

MATERIAL SOURCES

Olympia, Washington: A People's History; Drew W. Crooks (and others); 2009

Puget Sound Geography, original manuscript from T. T. Waterman, edited with additional material from Vi Hilbert, Jay Miller, and Zalmai Zahi; 2001

Native Olympia; Shanna Stevenson; 2012

What happened to the Steh-chass people? / Pat Rasmussen; 2014

Sent Out on the Tracks they Built: Sinophobia in Olympia, 1886 / Sarah Dougher, Nikki McClure; 1998

Rogues, Buffoons & Statesman; Gordon Newell; 1975

Never Knows History Cards of Thurston County, WA, vol, 1 & 2; Polly Calavara; 2012

How The West Was Once: A History Of West Olympia, Larry Smith / Jefferson Junior High School; 1974

ONLINE SOURCES

History of Olympia
olympiawa.gov/community/about-olympia/history-of-olympia-washington.aspx
olympiahistory.org/resources-for-researching-olympias-history

Regional geologic history
burkemuseum.org/geo_history_wa/

George Bush
historylink.org/index.cfm?DisplayPage=output.cfm&file_id=5645   http://www.historylink.org/File/10457

Oregon's African American exclusion laws

arcweb.sos.state.or.us/pages/exhibits/1857/before/slavery.htm

Rebecca Howard, Olympia African American pioneer
blackpast.org/aaw/howard-rebecca-groundage-1827-1881

Sister Cities / Kato City (formerly Yashiro), Japan
celebratejapan.org

Sister Cities / Santo Tomás, Nicaragua (association with Thurston County)
oly-wa.us/TSTSCA/

Sister Cities / Rafah (unofficial)
olyblog.net/olympiarafah-sister-city-project-faq

Bordeaux
  thurstontalk.com/2013/10/09/bordeaux-wa-last-remnants-thurston-county-ghost-town/

Musicians / bands:
  https://en.wikipedia.org/wiki/Music_of_Olympia

OFS
  https://en.wikipedia.org/wiki/Olympia_Film_Society
  olympiafilmsociety.org/about/capitoltheaterhistory/

Time magazine "Olympia, hippest city in the west" (July, 2000)

content.time.com/time/magazine/article/0,9171,11010008
07-51245,00.html

Ostrom's, Environmental
  ecy.wa.gov/news/2012/040.html

Food Co-op
  olympiafood.coop/join-us/about-ofc/history/

Garbage
  co.thurston.wa.us/solidwaste/garbage/garbage-warc.html

Carl Sagan on Ramtha
  positiveatheism.org/writ/saganbur.html

Pan and two mermaids removed from Procession of the Species
  https://diversityoftheprocession.wordpress.com

Chandu "CK" Patel, buys brewery for $4 million dollars chandukpatel-ck.com

Brewery Administrative Building fire doused with 1.5 million gallons of water
theolympian.com/news/local/article219735580.html

Train tunnel
olympiahistory.org/7th-avenue-tunnel/

Train station
historylink.org/index.cfm?DisplayPage=output.cfm&file_id=7929

Joseph Wohleb
dahp.wa.gov/learn-and-research/architect-biographies/joseph-h-wohleb

Pizza Time Robber
kiro7.com/news/suspected-serial-bank-robber-pizza-time-robber-arr/43517706

Mitchell Rupe
en.wikipedia.org/wiki/Mitchell_Rupe

Hollywood Bandit
historylink.org/index.cfm?DisplayPage=output.cfm&file_id=9043
en.wikipedia.org/wiki/Scott_Scurlock
stalkingseattle.blogspot.com/2012/04/hollywood-bank-robberies.html

OPD shoots Andre Thompson and Bryson Chaplin
socialistworker.org/2016/05/26/demanding-justice-for-andre-and-bryson

seattletimes.nwsource.com/archive/?date=19920220&slug
=1476788

OPD Officer Donald in another assault case:
  theolympian.com/news/local/crime/article26137630.html

**OPD shoots and kills José Ramírez Jiménez at a traffic
stop (2008)**
  olyblog.net/there-really-nobody-talking-about-josé-
ram%C3%ADrez-jiménez

**OPD accidentally kills Danny Spencer in police
custody (1989)**
  _community.seattletimes.nwsource.com/archive/?date=19
920220&slug=1476788

**OPD accidentally kills Stephan Edwards with tasers
(2002)**
  seattlepi.com/local/article/Three-have-died-in-
Washington-after-Taser-jolts-1160874.php

To support, learn more or get involved in
the work of ending racism in Olympia, visit:

olympiasurj.wordpress.com

BLOG:

comedicnonfiction.wordpress.com

CONTACT:

david@themartin.net

GET MORE COPIES:

BuyOlympia.com

MAKING SENSE
OF OLYMPIA

(book launch event at the Timberland Regional Library)

David Scherer Water has spent the last 31 years in Olympia. He has spent the last five writing this book, an offering to the place that has sustained and encouraged him. He appreciates feedback. This is David's third book following The Writer's Handbook, a self-help guide for aspiring authors and Twenty-Three, a collection of humorous poems written under the pen name Fezdak Clamchopbreath. Copies of his work can be purchased at local bookstores in Olympia and online at BuyOlympia.com.

Arrington de Dionyso is a musician and visual artist. His work ranges from _____ to _____. He also dabbles in _____. His work is available by searching his name.

Made in USA - Crawfordsville, IN
27513_9798352814406
10.04.2022 1447